Problem-based Learning:
How to Gain the Most from PBL

Donald R. Woods
McMaster University

Publisher: Donald R. Woods, Waterdown, ON, L0R 2H0
Printer: Seldon Griffin Graphics, Hamilton, ON L8P 4M3
Illustration and design: Janice O'Hoski
Cover design: M.P. Lehman and D.R. Woods
Distribution and sales: The Bookstore, McMaster University, Hamilton, ON. L8S 4L8
    FAX 905-572-7160 attention S. Hockridge; e-mail <Hocker@Bookstore.services.mcmaster.ca>

Problem-based Learning: How to Gain the Most from PBL

Translated into Japanese by Professor S. Shindo, published by Igaku-Shoin Ltd., Tokyo, 113-91, Japan, 2000
Instructors may wish to consult the guides:
Problem-based learning: helping your students gain the most from PBL 1995 ISBN 0-9698725-1-8
available on the www at http://www.chemeng.mcmaster.ca/innov1.htm and second edition published 1998

Problem-based learning: resources to gain the most from PBL 1995 ISBN 0-9698725-2-6
available on the www at http://www.chemeng.mcmaster.ca/innov1.htm and second printing of second edition, 1999

Canadian Cataloguing-in-Publication Data

Woods, Donald R.
    Problem-based Learning: How to Gain the Most from PBL

    Includes bibliographical references and index.
    ISBN 0-9698725-0-X

    1. Group problem solving. 2. Study skills. I. Title

LB2395.W66 1994   378.1 '7' 02812   C94-932125-7

Table of contents

3. Problem solving skills.

4. What is small group, problem-based learning?

5. Group skills.

6. What is self-directed, interdependent, small group, problem-based learning?

7. Self-directed, interdependent learning skills

8. What is self-assessed, self-directed, interdependent, small group, problem-based learning?

9. Self-assessment skills

10. Putting it all together.

Foreword

Don Woods has been committed to the challenge and excitement of problem-based learning for many years. He has put it in place in his own program, he has watched students struggling with the concepts in both traditional and problem-based settings and he probably knows as much about "PBL" as anyone around. Putting his thoughts on paper has always been associated with shuffling, organizing and diagramming information and this book is a clear reflection of the style which Don brings to his passion for the technology of learning.

Getting into this book either in small bites or in major meals is a fascinating venture into the way that he has thought about PBL for both individuals and for groups. If you want an in-depth look at what is involved in PBL then this book certainly gives you that look. Whether you be student or tutor there are stimulating and provocative examples, and thoughtful understanding and guidelines.

Many iterations of student learners have been thankful to Don for his enormous enthusiasm and this book brings some of that enthusiasm in a more portable and permanent format.

E. Kinsey M. Smith, M.D.
Associate Dean (Education),
McMaster Medical School, Hamilton, Canada

When I first heard about problem-based learning, I was full of enthusiasm. Here was a way (I reasoned) for my forestry students to learn many of the abilities necessary for competent professional practice while at the same time learning discipline-specific skills and knowledge. Imagine my surprise then, when some of my *lucky* students initially responded to PBL with somewhat less than my own enthusiasm.

In hindsight, it is easy to understand the reluctant students' point-of-view. After all, many students come to university after spending years learning to succeed in a mostly teacher-centered, discipline-based academic environment. But PBL requires students to be active, self-directed learners. It is no wonder that the shift to PBL represents a shocking, and sometimes unwelcome, change for some students.

Don Woods has recognized this problem and has undertaken to meet it head-on. Don's book, How to gain the most from Problem based learning, provides just the bridge that students need to understand PBL and to learn how best to benefit from it. I look forward to using this book with my forestry students.

Kenneth M. Brown,
Professor of Forestry,
Lakehead University, Thunder Bay, Canada

Having been involved with implementing problem-based curricula for the Occupational Therapy and Physiotherapy Programmes at McMaster University for the past four years I truly appreciate what Don has accomplished in his book.

Students think they know what they are getting into as they are offered admission to our programmes, however within weeks they start to struggle with the questions Don has addressed in his chapters. The book is easy to read and gives good examples as well as extensive bibliographies. I expect that this book will be used extensively in our programmes to help students cope better and get more out of their learning.

Professor Helen Saarinen, School of OT/PT, McMaster University, Hamilton, ON Canada

The profession of pharmacy is undergoing a dramatic transformation. The primary responsibilities of the pharmacist have traditionally focused ion the preparation and distribution of a drug product. Recently, the pharmacist's primary responsibilities have been refocused on the patient and the patient's drug therapy. Specifically, the pharmacist is assuming more responsibility for assuring, along with other health care professionals, the appropriate and safe use of medicinals. To do this, the pharmacist must be prepared to identify drug related problems, solve them and prevent them. Woods offers the pharmacist a very important and useful tool with which to be come proficient at these responsibilities. The newly defined role of the pharmacist lends itself to problem-based learning and Woods' text offers a good look at the skills needed to get proficient at it.

Professor Linda M. Strand, Pharmacy, University of Minnesota, St. Paul, MN., USA

There are many definitions of Problem-based Learning (PBL), and each of them makes a unique contribution to the field. This book on PBL, developed by Don Woods, makes two contributions. First, Woods provides a generic definition of PBL that is relevant and useful for learners from middle school age to adult, for diverse learning contexts (schools, college, work, medical, military, business, institutions of teacher education), and for learning organizations. Thus, the ideas and exercises in this book prepare learners for learning at home by themselves, for working in small groups assigned to solve various problems in various contexts, and for working through any of the structured models of PBL using rich case studies, standardized patients, goal-based scenarios and the like. Thus, whereas other models of PBL make their contribution by providing specific procedures, Woods makes a contribution by providing a model that anyone beyond primary school can use effectively. This model is practical, written in simple language with lots of tools and pointers to additional resources. I have used it myself, and I have recommended it to colleagues; If I were a teacher I would advise my students to use it.

Second, Woods deals with many social and emotional aspects of PBL that other models do not cover. Specifically, it assumes that changing the way you learn is painful and provides ideas and resources for addressing that pain. This book also speaks to the particular skills, concepts, and exercises for problem-based learning that is self-directed as well as group based. What is important here is that this book uses an array of text-based and visual strategies to facilitate learning and constructing powerful mental models. This book is well-written, well-organized, and walks the talk.

Beau Jones, North Central Regional Educational Laboratory, Oak Brook, IL., USA

Preface

This book is for students - students learning in a Problem-based Learning (PBL) environment. PBL improves learning; PBL is based on some of the best research in education and psychology; PBL is a preferred mode of learning by many students; PBL is one of the major success stories in education since the 1970s. You are fortunate, indeed, if you are learning via the PBL mode.

Your program in PBL may take one of many different forms: the business school "case study approach;" the "guided decision making/design approach," the McMaster Medical School PBL, a research project or other variations. What is similar for all of these variations is a *problem is used to drive the learning*. Whether your program is primarily a case study, a learning contract, guided design or the medical school PBL model, you can benefit from reading this book. Whether the PBL approach is used to facilitate your learning English, Psychology, Social Work, Law, Nursing, Pharmacy, Business, Architecture, Engineering, Dentistry, Police Work, Medicine, Chemistry or German, you can benefit by reading this book.

Much has been written for educators, teachers and administrators about how to implement PBL. This is the first book, that I am aware of, that is written for you, the student. The book has been developed, used and improved through feedback from students.

McMaster Medical School's approach to PBL has influenced what I do in the classroom. Hence, a more accurate description of the approach this book addresses most directly is described by the long-winded description "self-assessed, self-directed, interdependent, small group PBL". Nevertheless, my hope is that students wrestling with any form of PBL will benefit from this book.

What you will gain from this book is:

- An understanding of what to expect and a preparedness for how to cope effectively with the emotions you will encounter as you grapple with the new approach;.

- A framework to clarify the issues related to this PBL format and related to this process for learning.

- Skill and confidence in such *processing skills* as coping with change, problem solving, working effectively in a team, lifetime learning skills, and self-assessment.

- A cohesive overview of many diverse topics and of the "processing" skills that are needed to effectively use PBL and that provide valuable skills for living.

- Confidence that you can gain the most from your PBL experience.

Some will gain an understanding of why this approach might not suit them at this particular time. Even if you reach this decision, the journey will lead you in an exploration of skills important for everyday living: coping with change, problem solving, interpersonal skills, lifetime learning skills and self-awareness and self-assessment skills.

Use this book as a framework. This book introduces what you need-to-know about PBL, about coping with change or about the processing skills required when PBL is used. I have attempted to raise issues; ask you to reflect on your knowledge, skill and attitude about those issues; offer some activities to provide insight; but then, provide resources that you can use on a need-to-know basis. I have tried to model the PBL approach: describe a situation (in Chapters 1, 2, 4, 6 and 8), pose a problem (at the beginning of Chapters 1, 3, 5, 7, 9 and 10); ask, "What do you know already?" and then provide my list of issues. As your need dictates, you can skip to the next Chapter, or sample the specific issues.

Self-assessed, self-directed, interdependent, small group PBL demands (and develops) a host of complex skills. Most of you have skill in these. Sometimes we are unaware of that skill; we just "do it." Sometimes we unwittingly exhibit disruptive behaviour that impedes the learning. The book is organized to address the host of skills sequentially and layer skill upon skill. We use *successive approximation* to gradually build up the new knowledge and the processing skills. To some this may be frustrating because as you start PBL you need to apply **all** of the skills. You need to adjust to the newness and uncertainty of it all. You may feel stressed because you are not getting the familiar type of feedback that says, "You're doing OK!" Welcome to a change. Hence, Chapter 1 gives you a chance to look at change, in general.

For PBL, the first task is to define what we know, what we need to know, etc. We apply a systematic analysis and reflection. We create ideas; we monitor. In this book that set of mental skills is called "problem solving". Chapter 2 poses a problem. Chapter 3 offers a PBL opportunity to reflect on the issues and your needs as they relate to "problem solving".

For small group PBL, interpersonal and group skills are an asset. Chapter 4 poses the situation. Chapter 5 gives you a PBL opportunity to reflect on the issues and your needs for group skills.

Similarly, Chapters 6 and 7 consider self-directed, interdependent learning; Chapters 8 and 9, self-assessment. Chapter 10 puts it all together. In particular, Chapter 10 illustrates how to build up your skills gradually and successively in problem solving, group process, self-directed learning, self-assessment and your positive attitudes toward change.

The major themes in this book are:

- Knowledge and skill emerge through successive development.

- Have explicit, observable **goals** (for confidence, for managing stress, to remove the ambiguity in assessment, to function well in self-directed learning, to focus energies, and to successfully solve the real problem).

- Improving any skill does not occur if we just try doing it in an unstructured fashion. We improve by taking the skill apart into component tasks, doing the task, getting feedback to see how we performed the task, reflecting, learning from research evidence as to how the task should be done, setting goals and working toward those goals. This book outlines and applies this approach.

- Monitor and reflect on the processes; write in as journal. These activities help develop confidence in the skill.

- Have measurable criteria consistent with the goals.

- This book is a *framework* of issues and ideas; it lays out the major themes and their relationships. It addresses key issues. It gives resources for further study **as you need them**.

This book would not be possible without the advice, input, suggestions and encouragement from many, especially my students and my colleagues from McMaster Medical School. I thank the students in Chemical Engineering classes from 1985 onwards who helped me develop, evolve and adapt the SDL, PBL approach so that one instructor can facilitate this approach for class sizes of 40 plus students. The SDL, PBL approach is an integral part of the McMaster Problem Solving (MPS) program.

This MPS program, upon which this book is based, has been designed over the past 20 years to provide training in a broad range of over 50 skills related to problem solving, decision making, interpersonal relationships, group process, team building and lifetime learning. In its longer form, the program offers 120 hours of experiential training. For example, the skills outlined in Chapter 3, on a need-to-know basis, are developed, in the MPS program, through a structured set of 20 units. The key features are given in this book; details are available through specific MPS units.

The students in the "Theme School in New Materials," Andy Hrymak and Heather Wright helped me polish these notes. Vic Neufeld, Donna Mitchell, Elizabeth Brain, Luis Branda, Geoff Norman and Chris Woodward, all of the McMaster Medical School, generously shared their expertise with me. Alan Blizzard and Dale Roy, Instructional Development Centre, and my colleagues in Chemical Engineering, especially Andy Hrymak, Phil Wood, Bob Marshall, Les Shemilt, Cam Crowe, Terry Hoffman, Kim Woodhouse, Kyle Bouchard and Joe Wright aided, encouraged and supported the development of this approach.

Special thanks to Jean Crowe and Patricia Solomon, Occupational Therapy and Physical Therapy, McMaster University; Linda Muzzin and Wendy Duncan-Hewitt of the School of Pharmacy, University of Toronto; Neal Whitman, Director of Educational Development, the University of Utah; Marlene Roadruck, University of Central Queensland, Australia; Erik de Graaff, Delft University of Technology, the Netherlands and Geza Kardos, Carleton University for suggesting how to improve the text.

Erica Hawkins and Brian Decker helped me to publish this book.

I appreciate especially those who contributed to the foreword, offered suggestions and provided me with quotations about the book in the context of PBL: Kinsey Smith, Helen Saarinen, Linda Strand, Alistair Summerlee, Ken Brown, Beau Jones, Pierre Zundel, Charley Wales and Karin von Schilling.

Donald R. Woods
June 1994

Acknowledgements

Chapter 1.

p. 1-2. Figure 1-1. The grieving process. Adapted from *Networking: How to Enrich Your Life and Get Things Done* by D.R. Woods & S.D. Ormerod. Copyright ©1993 by Pfeiffer & Company, San Diego, CA. Used with permission.

p. 1-7. Table 1-3. Instructional Strategies Inventory. Joanne Gainen, 1987. Used with permission of the author. Teaching and Learning Center, Santa Clara University.

p. 1-6. Table 1-4. Learning Preference II. Fitch 1988. Adapted from Learning Environment Preferences scale by W.S. Moore copyright 1987 and Peggy Fitch copyright 1988. Used with permission of the Peggy Fitch, Dept. of Psychology, Central College, Pella, Iowa, 50219.

Chapter 3

p. 3-8. The Case of Jeremy Bridgewood. Reprinted from the 1990 Unit Four Health Care Problem, "Jeremy Bridgewood," HCP 104/88-90 courtesy of McMaster Faculty of Health Sciences, copyright 1990.

p. 3-19. Figure 3-6. Problem solver's processing of knowledge. from Larkin, 1976, reproduced with permission of Jill Larkin and reprinted with permission from *Chem. Eng. Ed.*, **27** (2), 81 (1993).

Chapter 5

p. 5-9, Table 5-1. Reprinted with permission from D.R. Woods and R.R. Marshall, copyright, 1990.

p. 5-12, Table 5-3 Sample agenda, reprinted with permission from Michelle Gretzinger and Kyle Bouchard.

Chapter 7

p. 7-5. Figure 7-6. Clement's mental modes of thinking. Used with permission from J.J. Clement, SRRI, University of Massachusetts, Amherst.

p. 7-9. Table 7-1. From Woods (1988). Reprinted with permission from *What Research Says to the Science Teacher, Volume 5: Problem Solving*. Copyright © 1989 by the National Science Teachers Association.

Chapter 9

p. 9-5. Table 9-3. Reprinted from the "1986 Unit One Handbook," Jose Venturelli, 1986 courtesy of McMaster Faculty of Health Sciences, copyright 1986.

1 *Are you ready for change?*

Why change?

Maria was happy as she was. She was getting good marks. She understood what was expected of her. She attended class, read the assigned reading, listened carefully to the prof to understand what was expected of her in the course. Of course, she handed in all her assignments on time.

Now, she attended her first class in the new format: problem-based, small group, self-directed learning. She asked her neighbour, "You mean we have to figure out what we need to know and then teach it to each other? I thought that was the responsibility of the prof! not me."

Dave replied, "From what I hear, this course is completely different from anything we have ever seen. I'm not sure I'm ready for this. Are you?"

We get very comfortable with routine. Many things happen when a change is made. If **we** initiate the change, we are impatient, excited and work hard to make it work. If the change is forced on us, then we basically *grieve*. We suffer most of the symptoms of someone who has lost a family member through death. Not perhaps as extreme, but similarly.

For this situation, what do you know already?

Perhaps you already have experienced change, or self-directed learning. If you know all of the issues and details for this situation already, skip to the next Chapter.

For this situation, what are the issues?

Some of the issues, for coping positively with a new adventure, are:

1. Be familiar with the *grieving* process so that you can positively work your way through the change.

2. Be able to apply the change process to the specific situation of using PBL: note the differences between the *old* and the *new* way of life.

3. Use stress and time management techniques to help work through the change.

4. Set goals for yourself about the "positive" things that can be learned from the new experience.

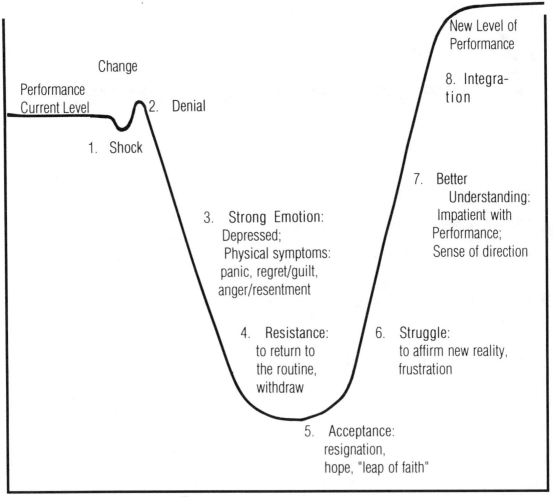

Figure 1-1 The *grieving* process as a model of how we cope with change

Each of these issues is considered in turn. You may wish to go directly to the section that answers your needs.

1.1. The "Grieving" Process for Coping with Change

Although each of us responds to change differently, in general, when we have a **mega** change, we are distressed and we usually have to work our way through most of a eight-step grieving process as we adjust to the *new*. Figure 1-1 illustrates the grieving

process. Taylor (1986) describes, in Table 1-1, the same process and elaborates on stages 5 through 8. Taylor developed her model to describe the disequilibrium of adult learners when they return to school. Also included in the bottom row of Table 1-1 are suggestions about how to work through the process. The eight stages are:

1. Shock: our performance decreases; we try to fathom what is happening. We are frustrated.

2. Denial: we try to cope by denying that this is really happening to us. We might work harder

Table 1-1 Working through the change process (based on Taylor, 1986)

1. Shock	3. Anxious, angry	5. Accept 6. Struggle	7. Sense of direction	Reflect	Organize	8. Integrate
Equilibrium becomes:	Disorientation		Explore		Reorient	
Discomfort; frustrated & confused because usual norms are gone.	Confusion Anxiety Tension Anger	Try to identify problem without blaming self or others.	You are on the right track but are unsure as to where it is going.	Reflect; desire to consolidate ideas & experience.	Light comes on! realize the change actually occurs within.	Share; satisfied with change and want to share.
	Crisis in confidence; negative self talk; self blame.		Relaxes & accepts change without having fully resolved it.			
	Withdraws from others associated with the source of confusion; no participation; aggression & hostility toward the tutor.	Reaffirms contract. Discovers others; helps identify productivity. Identifies cause of confusion or the problem.	Intuitive-guided-exploration. Focuses on the present time; "What will I do now?" Collaborates. Regains confidence.	Withdraws from collaborative activity. Privately reflects about the change process.	Personal start to synthesize ideas & experiences into perspective.	Shares major insight with someone.
How to proactively work your way through: realize that disorientation & anxiety are to be expected; study the change process.	Acknowledge your anger. It's normal. Resist the urge to withdraw.	Focus on defining the problem; see the *opportunity.*	Help bring the group together; use the change process & be positive.	Help others see the need for personal reflection (especially if all are not at the same stage in the change process).	Write reports about your experiences; share with others.	Allow time for feedback, to discuss, reflect and discover.

and hope that the instructor won't use PBL and will start to lecture again.

3. Strong emotion: we usually lose our confidence, have negative self-talk. Often we feel intense anger, especially toward the instructor (or the person who we see as being responsible for causing this change).

4. Resistance and withdrawal: we prefer to be alone and hope the change "goes away". "I think I'll miss today's PBL session."

5. Surrender and Acceptance: willing to accept; have a leap of faith that the new approach will work.

6. Struggle to reaffirm the new reality: exploration to define new opportunity.

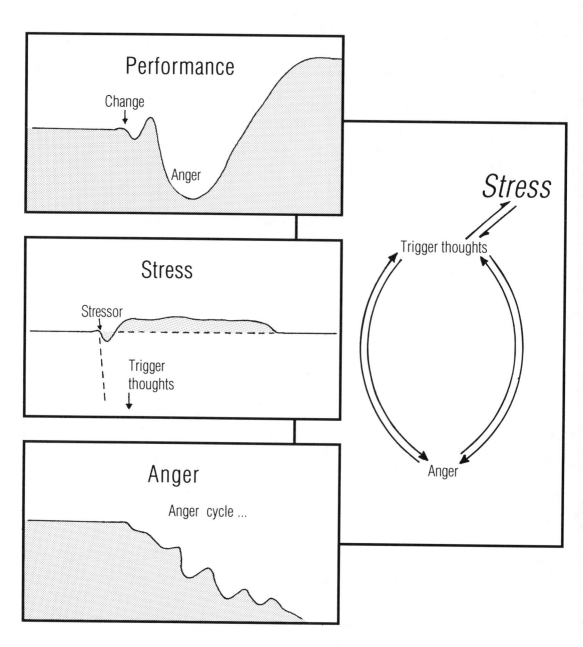

Figure 1-2 Change creates stress that triggers anger

7. Sense of direction: confidence returns; now we just have to "make this new approach work!" This is helped by reflection, organization and reorientation. The latter three are described in more details in Table 1-1.

8. Integration: new approach works!These feelings can accompany any change, no matter how small. The relationship between the grieving process, stress and anger is illustrated in Figure 1-2. Usually, a change triggers stress. Selye's (1975, 1978) model of stress shows the body's response/performance as a function of time. When the stressor hits, (for example, you experience a change) we have an initial "decrease" in performance. This corresponds to the "Shock" step in the model of change. Then, the body responds to create a positive "resistance stage" that helps us cope until we return to "normal performance". Often, the initial stressor also triggers self-talk that feeds anger. The self-talk triggers anger which causes more self-talk. Anger and frustration increase. The performance cycles downwards as all our efforts go to feeding the anger. This interaction is illustrated in Figure 1-2. Although we may have little control over the change ("This course is given in the PBL format."), how to manage the accompanying stress and anger is controllable.

In summary, we can describe typical emotions you will probably feel during a change. Having these feelings is natural. Realize where you are in the process and systematically work your way through it. You might not experience all of the emotions. You may experience them in different sequences. However, *usually* most of them are there. Become comfortable working through the change process.

If you need more on the general concepts about coping with change and the grieving process, then take time to consult such sources as Bridges (1980, 1991), Woods and Ormerod (1993) and Westberg (1971) and to discuss your findings with your friends. More ideas about managing stress, time management, and managing anger are given in

Section 1.3. Section 1.4 gives suggestions about motivation.

1.2 Identifying the Key Differences Between the "Old" and the "New" as They Apply to PBL .

Section 1.1 described the change process in general. This will help you in lifetime living. But what about the specific situation of learning by PBL? Much has changed in the PBL approach: the role of the teacher, the role of the student, the role of examinations, and general expectations. Perry, in his model of development, described each of these issues. Table 1-2 gives his list. In PBL, students find that the conditions given in column 5 apply. That is, instead of thinking all knowledge is known (Level 2) they realize that different knowledge applies to different situations. Instead of viewing the student's role as a Level 2 view of "to receive," they realize their responsibility is to identify the conditions specific to *this problem* and to choose the most pertinent ideas. What most students usually hold is a mix between Level 2 and 4. That is, they might be at level 4 concerning their attitude toward assessment, but at level 2, for the role of the student.

Where are you in terms of attitude toward learning? Tables 1-3 and 1-4 give example inventories to help you reflect on your attitudes. Is there a difference for you between the "new expectation" of column 5 and your response to the inventories that might reflect your "old approach" to learning? If there is a difference, then you will experience change. However now you know more about the conditions of that change so that you can work your way through the change process more effectively.

1.3 Use Stress, Time and Anger Management Techniques to Help.

Stress accompanies most change. Indeed, change usually triggers stress, as illustrated in Figure 1-2. Stress can debilitate you. In particular, student in a PBL program often encounter distress about week

Table 1-2 Perry's model of attitude toward learning (Perry, 1970)

View toward	Perry's scale			
	1-2	3	4	5
Knowledge	All knowledge is known.	Most is known but there are some fuzzy areas.	Some is known; no certainty; anything goes.	Different knowledge is needed in different contexts.
Answers to problems	Either right or wrong.		My answer is as good as yours.	No absolute truth; answers are relative but good answers exist once the conditions are known.
Teacher, tutor, instructor	Instructor and books know the truth.	Role is to tell us how to learn.	Role is as models; but they can be completely discounted.	Role is to be a guide and source of expertise.
Student's role	To receive.	To work hard and to learn how to learn.	To think for yourself; independent thought is good.	To identify the conditions; to choose the best ideas.
Assessment	Worried if exam format is fuzzy. Asks, "What do you expect?" Equate bad grades with bad person.	Is the key issue. Quantity and fairness. Hard work = good mark.	Independent ideas equal good mark. Can separate assessment of work from personal worth.	Seek positive and negative feedback on assessment.
Preferred task	Memorize definitions.	Compare and contrast.	Analysis.	Synthesis. Relate ideas between contexts.
Difficult task	Decide which of two conflicting authorities is correct. Tell me.	Focus on the "process" and not on the answer.	Provide evidence to support claims. Learning to listen to authority again.	Decide on which conditions apply.

3 to 4: they wonder, "Am I learning anything?" "Am I learning the right thing?" "How am I doing?" Remind yourself that you have been successful in the past; you will succeed in the future. Listed here is a succinct summary of how to manage stress, time and anger. Use this as a reminder. Use this as a guide to improvement. Use this as a source of further reading if you need it.

For **stress management** Table 1-5 lists a range of techniques. You might find it helpful to remind yourself of some of these techniques, and to monitor your use of them. If you need more on this topic, take time to read such resources as Hanson (1985) and Meichenbaum (1983) or the resources from the McMaster Problem Solving program supporting this book, MPS **5**.

Related to stress management are time management and anger management. You probably are skilled at these already. Here is a succinct reminder of the key ideas.

For **time management**, the keys seem to be:
1. Know and value yourself.
2. Be proactive, see yourself as being in charge of your life.

Table 1-3 Inventory of learning preference (Gainen, 1987) used with permission)

For each of the items listed, circle the one option that best describes the kind of course, or learning environment, that you prefer.

1. Instruction focuses primarily on:
    A. Conveying facts, concepts, skills and/or standardized procedures.
    B. Sharing or clarifying ideas, experiences and/or opinions.
    C. Explaining theories and/or issues.
    D. Evaluating theories and/or issues.

2. The course covers:
    A. A standardized set of topics from a single textbook.
    B. Topics selected according to the instructor's preference.
    C. Topics selected by the instructor with input from students.
    D. Topics chosen by students to reflect their interests.

3. The course uses:
    A. Instructional methods for each topic selected by the instructor and used by all students.
    B. A variety of instructional options for each topic (e.g.individualized instruction, media-supported instruction, research papers, group work); students can select the approach they prefer.
    C. Instructional methods developed in consultation with students to reflect their preferred modes of learning.
    D. Instructional methods proposed and implemented by the students and supervised by the instructor.

4. How do you prefer the course content to be organized?
    A. The course covers a single unified approach to the subject.
    B. The course covers two or three themes or perspectives on the topic.
    C. The course presents a variety of themes or perspectives on the topic, some of which are in opposition to each other.
    D. The course dramatizes the differences between major perspectives on the topic.

5. Do you prefer instructors who:
    A. Stick close to the most widely-accepted view of the subject?
    B. Give equal treatment to a variety of perspectives, emphasizing that they are all equally valid and important?
    C. Compare various perspectives systematically to identify their strengths and weaknesses?
    D. Show students how to analyze the material so they can arrive at their own perspectives on the topic?

6. Do you prefer instructors who use:
    A. Formal lectures, using examples and visual aids whenever possible; or lectures with time for questions?
    B. A mix of lecture and discussion with opportunities for students to express their opinions?
    C. Discussion or exercises in which the students explore conceptual relationships and implications of the topic?
    D. Exercises or activities that require students to use course material to address problems or issues in the field?

7. Do you prefer grades to be based primarily on:
    A. Multiple choice or short answer, objective examinations?
    B. A mix of objective examinations and short assignments in which students express their opinions on the subject?
    C. A few assignments and/or exams that require students to pursue an aspect of the subject in some depth?
    D. Assignments or exams that require students to synthesize material from the course?

8. In your preferred course, what must students do primarily to succeed?
    A. Learn important facts, skills, procedures and/or concepts.
    B. Fully understand two or more theoretical perspectives.
    C. Relate (compare, contrast, analyze or evaluate) several theories, themes or methodologies; or analyze issues or solve unfamiliar problems using course concepts.
    D. Formulate, and present arguments for a position, or design a system, or develop a new approach to a problem in the field, integrating concepts and perspectives from the course.

SUM: A _____   B _____   C _____   D _____

Table 1-4 Moore and Fitch inventory for learning preference, LP-II (Fitch, 1988, used with permission)
Each of us has an ideal learning environment. Think of how you learn best. Try **not** to focus on one particular course or one particular instructor. Focus on their significance in an **ideal** learning environment for you.

You have **10** check marks to distribute among 34 questions. Put a check mark in the * column next to the statement that best describes your ideal learning environment. The code column is for easy reference when we discuss the inventory.

code	**My ideal learning environment:**
63	would provide assignments with practical everyday applications.
22	would have the professor give me all the theory and information I need to know.
74	would be where I would have a lot of control over the course content and class discussion.
72	would be where I take effective notes on what is presented in class and reproduce that information on tests.
13	would emphasize class discussion but I would expect the professor to tell us the right answer.
24	would be where I have my own opinions and I can think for myself.
53	include grading that is by a prearranged point system (for homework, tests, final) since I think that is most fair.
42	would include straightforward, not "tricky" tests, covering only what has been taught and nothing else.
64	would let me learn on my own because I hate being spoofed by professors.
73	would be where the professor doesn't tell me the answers; rather he/she shows me how to find the answers for myself.
95	would provide a flexible class where I can explore independent learning options.
44	is where my opinion counts, but I have to support it with factual evidence.
52	would be where the professor is an expert who knows all the answers.
83	would provide experiences and material that is relevant to what I need to know later.
15	would be where learning is a mutual experience where I contribute to the teaching and learning in class.
12	would have the focus on having the right answers rather than on discussing methods on how to solve problems.
45	would value my classmates as sources of information, not only as companions.
14	would reward me with high grades for independent thought.
82	would be where the professor provides me with clear directions and guidance for all course activities and assignments.
65	would take learning seriously and be where I feel personally motivated to learn the subject.
33	would reward me with good grades when I worked hard to learn the material.
55	would provide me with a professor who is a source of expertise only in a particular subject area.
54	would let me learn from my classmates and peers.
35	would provide a classroom atmosphere of exploring and debating new ideas.
43	would encourage me to learn using lots of different learning methods.
84	would allow peers the right to have their own opinions.
25	would include exams and assessment as part of the learning process.
62	would be lectures since I can get the information I need to know most efficiently.
23	would have a professor who was not just an instructor, but more an explainer, entertainer and friend.
34	would be a "free-flowing" class that does not follow a strict outline.
85	would provide a workshop or seminar atmosphere so that we can exchange ideas and evaluate our own perspectives on the subject matter.
93	would provide a relaxed atmosphere where discussion is encouraged.
32	would be where I could listen intently to the professor and not to classmates and peers for answers to questions.
75	would be where I can make connections among various subject areas and am encouraged to construct an adequate argument.

Table 1-5 Monitoring checklist for stress management

Ideas	Not for me	Might work	OK	Use now
1. Worry only about things over which you have control				
2. Take care of yourself: exercise, eat and sleep regularly				
3. Use destimulating activities: deep breathing, muscle relaxation				
4. Use positive, **not** negative, self-talk: Rate your self-talk: don't know very negative neutral very positive				
5. Plan ahead				
6. Rename the stressful event: don't know use anxious name neutral "thing" positive				
7. Have a support system of family and friends. don't know have none few some many Have support system of traditions don't know have none few some many				
8. Use positive addictions that take your mind away to another world: music, hot bath, crafts, hobbies				
9. Be decisive				
10. Put it into perspective: "It's not the end of the world!"				
11. Use role models who have succeeded. don't know have none few some many				
Current stress: Symptoms	none	few	some	many
As measured by Holmes-Rahe (1967) or Holmes Gmelch (1983)	<100	101-300	301-500	>501

3.   Have goals.

The specific ways to put this all together are:

1.   Be proactive; don't "hope" it will all work out; don't say "what will be will be." Take charge of your self and your goals!

2.   Have personal goals and task or short term goals. See where the short-term goals fit into the long term goals. My personal goals are "to treat everyone with respect and to apply the golden rule"; my shorter term goal is to pass this year with a B-; my immediate goal is to complete the three assignments this week.

3. Prioritize your personal goals and the short term goal.

4. Plan and anticipate problems.

5. Address both the task and morale issue: "What tasks need to be done?" "How do I reward and keep myself motivated?"

6. Keep a balance in your life; manage stress.

7. Use a problem solving approach.

The mechanics of how we manage time include:

1. Know your overall personal goals.

2. List the tasks to be done and ensure that we **really** know what is expected. "What are we supposed to produce?" Apply the principle of successive approximation. This principle is described in Chapter 2.

3. Keep all the tasks in perspective, with each other, and with your overall personal goals. Prioritize! "Is it worth completing this assignment and getting a high if it means losing your best friend and getting sick because you don't get enough sleep?"

4. Assess the amount of time (and resources) you have available and determine how best to use them. Iterate with the previous three items and reassess. Determine what really can be done.

5. Learn to say **NO!**

6. Develop a realistic plan and anticipate potential problems. Think of how you will cope with these.

7. Develop methods for monitoring, giving yourself feedback, providing morale boosts, communicating with yourself, making changes to your plan.

If you need more on this topic, my favourite resource for time management is Covey (1990).

You might read the resources from the McMaster Problem Solving program supporting this book, MPS **17**.

Anger is probably the most destructive of all of the emotions that characterize the change process. The anger may be directed toward yourself; it may be directed toward those imposing change on you. It may be directed at innocent bystanders who were in the wrong place at the wrong time. Here is what research suggests about anger (McKay, Rogers and McKay, 1989; Meichenbaum 1983; Hankins and Hankins, 1988)

1. **You** choose to be angry. Anger is not biologically based or inherited; anger is controllable.

2. You can't *make* other people change or interact with you differently; you can change how you react.

3. Anger costs too much. Relieving your feelings by venting anger (blasting the other person) rarely leads to any real relief or lasting catharsis. It leads instead to more anger, tension and arousal. Anger costs through deterioration of your personal health and through loss of friends. Inability to express or control anger contributes to hypertension; expressing anger leads to high blood pressure.

4. Stress doesn't cause anger; stress is the fuel of anger. We choose to be angry because we choose to respond to self-talk "triggers" that start the anger cycle as illustrated in Figure 1-2. Indeed, McKay et al. (1989) suggest that the sole function of anger is to *stop stress* by discharging or blocking awareness of stressful triggers.

5. The self-talk triggers for anger are ones that identify *someone else* as being responsible. We say to ourself, "They should have done...." "Who did this to me?", "I'm a victim.." The two classes of self-talk triggers are: the **"shoulds"** and the **"blamers"**.

Thus, to manage anger, stop the self-talk.
If you need more on managing anger, McKay, Rogers and McKay (1989) offer good examples and advice. The McMaster Problem Solving program materials to complement this text are the MPS **52**, "Interpersonal skills."

1.4 Set Goals, Do Commitment Charting, Monitor Progress and be Motivated

To see potential "good" in the change, we should:

1. Identify the current or "from" situation. What was life like? What were we comfortable doing? Table 1-6 can be used for this purpose.

2. Identify the future or "to" situation. What will life be like?

3. Brainstorm positive, negatives and interesting outcomes from the opportunity.

4. Set goals for progress so that we make the most of the opportunity.

5. Monitor progress.

6. Use commitment charting to guide you in understanding your priorities and your time commitment you can apply to this PBL activity. An example commitment chart is given in Figure 1-3. On your own, record your priority and the numbers of hours per week you can commit. If you are working in a group, ask all to complete this information privately. Then share. Explore the implications for the group. (In my view, commitment charting is **not** a method to decide how a "grade" should be allocated. I think such a goal is inappropriate in the context of team work. The team gets the rewards and not individuals. Rather, use commitment charting to understand and respect where other team members are coming from. This helps minimize potential conflict over the issue, "Is everyone pulling their weight on this team?") Beckhard and Harris (1987) give more on commitment charting.

Table 1-6 Worksheet to see opportunities

Change from:			
Issue:	from:	to:	opportunity:

This team activity has the following priority considering all of my other commitments:

100　　highest priority

90

80

70

60

50

40

30

20

10

0　　zero priority

The **usual** amount of time I can spend is

_____ h per 　 week, day, month (circle)

The **minimum** amount of time I can spend is

_____ h per 　 week, day, month (circle)

The **maximum** amount of time I can spend is

_____ h per 　 week, day, month (circle)

Figure 1-3 Commitment charting

Here are some general suggestions for coping with change effectively:

1. Be patient. Take your time. The external part of your life may have changed abruptly. You have arrived in a new environment. Allow time for your inner-self to adjust.

2. Arrange temporary structures. Develop ways of carrying on while the inner reorientation is taking place.

3. Don't act just for the sake of action. Don't lash out at others. Curtail rash actions.

4. Recognize the change process. Congratulate yourself as you internally work your way through each stage. Recognize why you are uncomfortable and frustrated; understand the transition process. Expect times of anxiety and anger. Expect others to feel threatened and unclear as to how to "handle you"; expect old fears to be awakened.

5. Apply your reliable stress management techniques. Take care of yourself in little ways. Pamper yourself.

6. Use your network. Get someone to talk to.

In summary, proactively address your attitudes toward PBL and address the roller-coaster of emotions that usually accompany starting something new. You are ready for PBL!

1.5 Summary

Background ideas were given about change. Misconceptions are given about change. The grieving process model and Taylor's model describe the feelings one is likely to encounter during the change process.

The suggested tactics for managing change include be aware of the change process and be motivated to work your way through the process (by setting goals and managing resistance).

1-6: References:

Beckhard, R. and Harris, R.T. (1987) "Organizational Transitions: Managing Complex Change," 2nd ed Addison Wesley, Reading MA.

Billings, A.G., and R.H. Moos (1981) "The Role of Coping Responses and Social Resources in Attenuating the Stress of Life Events," J. Behavioral Medicine, 4, 2, 139-141.

Bridges, W. (1980) "Transitions: making sense of life's changes," Addison Wesley; Reading, MA.

Bridges, W. (1991) "Managing Transitions: making the most of change," Addison Wesley; Reading, MA.

Covey, S.R. (1990) "The 7 Habits of Highly Effective People," Fireside Book, Simon and Schuster, New York, NY.

Daitz, B. "Learning Medicine," The University of New Mexico School of Medicine, 2400 Tucker Dr., Albuquerque, NM 87131. [videotape]

Fitch, Peggy (1988) personal communication.

Gainen, J. (1987) "Instructional Strategies Inventory," personal communication, Center for Teaching Effectiveness, University of Delaware.

Hankins, G. and C. Hankins (1988) "Prescription for Anger," Warner Books, New York, NY.

Hanson, P.G. (1985) "The Joy of Stress," Andrews, McMeel & Parker, Kansas City.

Holmes, T.H. and Rahe, R.H. (1967) "The Social Readjustment Rating Scale," J. of Psychosomatic Research, Aug, 213-218.

Holmes-Gmelch (1983) Personal communication from W. Gmelch, Washington State University, Pullman, WA.

McKay, M., P.D. Rogers and J. McKay (1989) "When Anger Hurts: quieting the storm within," New Harbinger Publications, Oakland, CA.

Meichenbaum, D. (1983) "Coping with Stress," J. Wiley and Sons, Toronto, ON.

Moore, W.S. (1987) "Learning Environment Preferences," Center for Applications of Developmental Instruction,

MPS 5 (1993) "Engage: "I want to and I can!," McMaster Problem Solving program, Department of Chemical Engineering, McMaster University, Hamilton, ON.

MPS 17 (1993) "Time management," McMaster Problem Solving program, Department of Chemical Engineering, McMaster University, Hamilton, ON.

MPS 52 (1993) "Interpersonal Skills," McMaster Problem Solving program, Department of Chemical Engineering, McMaster University, Hamilton, ON.

Perry, W.G., Jr. (1970) "Forms of Intellectual and Ethical Development in the College Years: a scheme," Holt Rinehart and Winston, New York, NY.

Selye, H. (1975) "Stress without distress," McClelland Stewart Ltd., Toronto, ON.

Selye, H. (1978) "The Stress of Life," 2nd edition, McGraw Hill, New York, NY.

Suzuki, D. "Doctors of Tomorrow" from the CBC program "The Nature of Things," Filmaker's Library, 124 East 40th St., New York, NY 10016.

Taylor, M. (1986) "Learning for Self-direction in the Classroom: the pattern of a transition process," Studies in Higher Education, 11, 55.

Wales, Charley (1974) "Guided Design," Center for Guided Design, University of West Virginia, Morgantown, WV [videotape]

Westberg, G.E. (1971) "Good Grief," Fortress Press, Philadelphia, PA.

Woods, D.R. (1993a) "Participation is More than Attendance," Department of Chemical Engineering, McMaster University, Hamilton, ON.

Woods, D.R. (1993b) "The MPS SDL program," Department of Chemical Engineering, McMaster University, Hamilton ON. [videotape]

Woods, D.R. and S.D. Ormerod (1993) "Networking: how to enrich your life and get things done," Pfeiffer and Co., San Diego, CA.

1.7 Exercises

1.1 For the case "Why change?", visualize what you might say to Maria to help her understand about change.

1.2 The Billings-Moos inventory (1981) can give you some idea of how you have coped with change this past year. You might wish to complete that inventory and reflect on the implications.

1.3 Complete the opportunity charting in Table 1-6. What are the implications for you personally? Monitor the time you actually spend during a 2 week period.

1.4 As a group of five just getting started in a PBL program, the group members completed the commitment charting activity and shared

the following results for % priority and hours per week:

- Tanya	60%	8 h
- Adam	80%	15 h
- Troy	10%	3 h
- Sharif	50%	6 h
- Nicole	55%	5 h

Negotiate how you would handle the variability in:
a. background preparation and expectation,
b. rewards or marks (if there is a mark given to the PBL activity).
c. other.

1.5 Some might like to "get a mark for participation". Devise a method for giving feedback to each other about the quality of participation. For some ideas see Woods (1993a).

1.6 Motivation. In some contexts you are taking PBL courses concurrently with traditional lecture-based, marks oriented, and with assignments due each week. PBL offers a lot of freedom, and you tend to work harder and learn more in PBL **unless** there is a crunch with deadlines in the other courses. Do a force-field diagram to make explicit the temptations that, if followed, would reduce your effectiveness in and your contribution to PBL. (Kurt Lewin's force-field approach is illustrated in University Associates Annual '73, p 111 or Structured Experiences, II, p 79. published by University Associates, San Diego, CA.) These might include: "topic in PBL is too ambitious for the time available," or "assignment worth 15% is due in lecture course," and "fascinating topic in PBL that is very complex to understand."
Develop strategies to cope effectively with these temptations.

1.7 Different videotapes are available to see PBL in action. In medical school contexts, use Daitz or Suzuki. For engineering contexts, use Wales or Woods (1993b). Check with your librarian or your tutor about the availability of these videotapes.

2 What is problem-based learning?

Professor Case asks:

> "Here's a toaster that isn't working, fix it! or better still, improve it."

On the other hand, Professor English begins:

> "Today we are going to study the flow of electricity through metals, then we'll look at..."

Professor Case is using a *problem* situation to drive the learning. She doesn't tell us the name of the course, the textbook we should purchase or what we have to study. All we know is that we need to discover:

- What we need to know about the fundamentals relating to what makes a toaster work, and

- How we can apply that new knowledge to solve the posed problem.

Professor English outlines the *subject* discipline and its structure to drive the learning. He usually does it in the context of the name of the course with an assigned textbook. He, like Professor Case, will

also use problems, but in a different way. The problems may be posed and a solution given by Professor English to illustrate how to apply the knowledge.

Both approaches use **problems** but for two completely different reasons. Case uses problems to drive the learning. English uses problems to illustrate how to use the knowledge **after** you have learned it.

In this Chapter we define problem-based learning, explore the advantages and disadvantages of PBL, and suggest how to make the most of the PBL format.

2.1 What Is PBL?

You would be amazed to realize how much you *already* know about a subject. Yet, subject-based learning assumes you know very little and proceeds to lay out the information in a preselected sequence. Although, you may already know some of it, you are forced to read it all "in case you miss something." Subject-based learning presents what the teacher (or text author) thinks you need to know. In problem-based learning, your task is to discover what **you** need to know to address the "problem posed." Figure 2-1 contrasts subject-based with problem-based learning.

PBL can be a research project, a case method, a design project, a trouble-shooting situation, a clinical encounter, an educational approach called Guided Design, or a self-directed, self-assessed, small learning group. The options often depend on who is responsible for directing the activity: teacher-directed or student-directed. Table 2-1 illustrates the interaction between how we organize the subject and how we distribute the responsibility. PBL addresses how we organize the subject. Thus, the traditional lecture is "subject-based" and "teacher-directed." Case studies can be "problem-based" and, often, are "teacher-directed." The variation of PBL that is the focus of this book is "small group, self-directed PBL" which is "problem-based" and "student-directed."

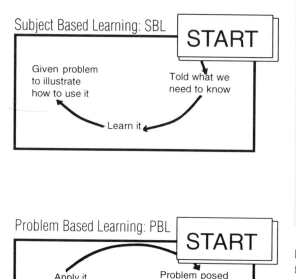

Figure 2-1 Subject-based versus PBL

Eight tasks

1. Explore the problem, create hypotheses, identify issues. Elaborate.

2. Try to solve the problem with what you currently know. From this will come a clearer idea of what you know already that is pertinent.

3. Identify what you do **not** know and therefore what you need to know because your lack of that knowledge is impeding the solution of the problem.

4. Prioritize the learning needs, set learning goals and objectives, and allocate resources so that you know what is expected of you by when. For a group, members can identify which tasks each will do.

5. Self-study and preparation.

6. For a group, share the new knowledge effectively so that all the group learn the information.

7. Apply the knowledge to solve the problem.

8. Give yourself feedback by assessing the new knowledge, the problem solution and the effectiveness of the process used. Reflect on the process.

Regardless of who owns the responsibility, the key for PBL is that the focus is to use a problem situation to drive the learning activities on a need-to-know basis. Eight tasks to guide you through the experience of PBL are given in box to the right. These tasks, especially numbers 4 and 6, vary depending on whether you are using PBL as an individual or as a group. As an individual you would omit task 6.

Table 2-1 Options for learning

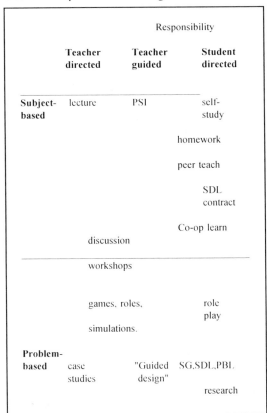

	Responsibility		
	Teacher directed	**Teacher guided**	**Student directed**
Subject-based	lecture	PSI	self-study
			homework
			peer teach
			SDL contract
			Co-op learn
	discussion		
	workshops		
	games, roles, simulations.		role play
Problem-based	case studies	"Guided design"	SG,SDL,PBL research

2.2 Advantages and Disadvantages

The advantages and disadvantages are as follows.

2.2-1 Advantages of PBL

Having a problem at the beginning provides a concrete application and motivates us. The way we memorize the knowledge provides links and experiences that help us recall and use the knowledge at a future time. Specifically, embedding the knowledge, old and new, in the context of the problem helps us to integrate the knowledge. Thus, problem-based learning helps us to learn and comprehend new material far better than subject-based learning. Problem-based learning usually synthesizes a broad range of subjects and topics.

This is highlighted in Figure 2-2 for a problem in criminology in the Case of the Dinged Stop Sign.

> Case of the Dinged Stop Sign.
>
> Detective Frank Kolaski needs to identify exactly where the 1.7 m tall suspect Bozo Armstrong was standing when the shots were fired. He located a bullet in a telephone pole at an angle of 60° with an apparent dimple or ding in a metal stop sign 2.3 m above the street. Bozo claims he was standing facing the stop sign but 50 m away from it and at an angle of 60° the other side of the pole. The bullet hole was 3.2 m off the ground. The telephone pole is 10 m away from the stop sign.

In traditional education, teachers would *lecture* on Geometry and we would have a full course in Geometry. Then, we would have a course in Physics, and Ballistics, and Materials, and Criminology, and Psychology. When we had completed all those courses we might encounter the "Case of the Dinged Stop Sign." As we worked on this problem we would be applying selected portions from each of those six courses. Contrast this with PBL where we have **not** had any courses. From our analysis of the problem we would identify that we need to know something from each course. We might see connections across courses. Thus, in PBL we take a horizontal collection of information that is pertinent to this problem. We learn a little about each and synthesize it to solve the problem. Figure 2-2a illustrates the status after one problem. Figure 2-2b shows us part way through a course. In the subject-based approach, we might have completed courses in Geometry and Physics. We know a lot about these two; we know nothing about the others. In the PBL approach, our next problem might be the Case of the torpedoed cruiser. Such a problem would extend, in Geometry, our knowledge about the shape of ships; in Physics, about buoyancy. Thus, the problems are used to build up ever-enriching layers of new knowledge across disciplines. This layering process is illustrated in Figure 2-3 where concepts B are layered on concepts A. This idea of building up our knowledge successively is an important concept to master. We will call it the principle of successive development.

2.2-2 Disadvantages of PBL

The first apparent disadvantage is that you may be uncomfortable with PBL simply because you are so used to subject-based learning. Traditionally, we learn Geometry, English, Chemistry, Mathematics. Traditionally, we pass exams in Physics, Biology and French. We are not used to studying "The Case of the Dinged Stop Sign" or "The Case of Harry Strange."

The second apparent disadvantage is that sometimes in PBL it seems that the amount we learn from each case is less and that we would like to have learned more depth. In PBL we are learning new knowledge by successively adding more depth with each new problem we solve. That is, for the **first** problem we consider, our tendency is to "want to know it all." But we can't! If we try, we run out of resources. For example, in the case of the "Dinged Stop Sign," our tendency is to **want** to know everything about geometry, everything about particle mechanics, everything about ballistics, everything about materials, everything about criminology and everything about psychology. And all in 3 minutes! We must learn to limit that tendency of **wanting** to know everything from one problem. Instead, we can begin to move modestly by using what we **need** to know for this particular problem. (Enrichment is possible after the problem has be completed; but we must not get mired down in details to such an extent that we don't solve the case.) This challenge will be more acute for those of us whose personal learning style prefers the details. (We discuss personal style and its implications in Chapters 5 and 7. If you need to know something more about it right now, the annotated index will lead you to the information.)

A third apparent "disadvantage" is that with PBL we take longer to learn the same subject content. But, in fact, this illusion of "wasted time" is related to two factors:

i) We like the PBL format so much that we often elect to learn more depth than is needed at that time. We learn because we are interested; not to pass an exam.

ii) We are developing other skills besides acquiring knowledge. We are applying our problem solving skills, inquiry skills and thinking skills explicitly. We are not merely memorizing what some else tells us to memorize.

Finally, a fourth challenge is that the PBL approach assumes that we are good at problem solving; that we are aware of our problem solving processes. We may not be, at first. Hence, we need to conscientiously develop that skill as we learn the "subject knowledge."

2.3 Making the Most of the PBL Format

From a learning viewpoint, all research points to the advantage of the PBL format. We learn more, we learn better and the knowledge is integrated and memorized in more accessible and applicable

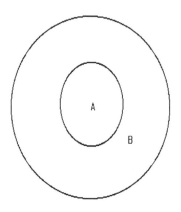

Figure 2-3 Build up knowledge successively in ever-enriching layers

a. After the first Case

Geometry	Physics	Ballistics	Materials	Criminology	Psychology
Case 1: 3D angles	trajectory motion, Newton's laws, reflection	type of armament, type of bullet, speed, effect of weather	stop sign, would the bullet go through or bounce off? materials for bullet, could any striations on the bullet after it had bounced off a sign be matched with a gun?	would this criminal use a gun, motives, details of the crime scene	could Frank fool Bozo into believing he could get valuable evidence from this situation and wring a confession from Bozo?
full course on geometry	full course on physics				

b. After several Cases

Geometry	Physics	Ballistics	Materials	Criminology	Psychology
Case 1: 3D angles	trajectory motion, Newton's laws, reflection	type of armament, type of bullet, speed, effect of weather	stop sign, would the bullet go through or bounce off? materials for bullet, could any striations on the bullet after it had bounced off a sign be matched with a gun?	would this criminal use a gun, motives, details of the crime scene	could Frank fool Bozo into believing he could get valuable evidence from this situation and wring a confession from Bozo?
Case 2:					
Case 3:					
full course on geometry	full course on physics				

Figure 2-2 Comparing Subject-based with PBL

forms. However, to make the most of this approach, we need to reflect on our skill at problem solving.

We also need to resist the crutch of returning to the familiar subject-based format.

2.4 Summary

Problem-based learning uses a posed problem to drive the learning. From our analysis of the problem, we define what information is pertinent to solve the problem, identify the new knowledge we need, learn the new knowledge and then apply it to solve the problem. We benefit most from the experience, if we reflect on the learning process afterwards.

Videotapes are available that demonstrate PBL in action. For medical school contexts, consult Daitz or Suzuki. I prefer the former. For engineering contexts, use Wales or Woods.

2.5 References

Daitz, B. (undated) "Learning Medicine," The University of New Mexico School of Medicine, 2400 Tucker Dr., Albuquerque, NM 87131.

Kardos, G. (1971) ECL-174 "To Find a Bullet," Center for Case Studies in Engineering, Rose Hulman Institute of Technology, Terra Haute, IN 47803-3999

Suzuki, D. (undated) "Doctors of Tomorrow" from the CBC program "The Nature of Things," Filmaker's Library, 124 East 40th St., New York, NY 10016.

Wales, Charley (1974) "Guided Design," Center for Guided Design, University of West Virginia, Morgantown, WV.

Woods, D.R. (1993) "The MPS SDL program," 24 min videotape, Department of Chemical Engineering, McMaster University, Hamilton, ON.

2.6 Exercises

2.1 For the Case of the Dinged Stop Sign, the problem statement was short. Yet, in Figure 2-2, at least six different issues were expected. For example, the words ." . needs to know exactly where..," "Detective" and "suspect" lead to the subjects of criminology and psychology. Would you prefer that the initial problems statement be more detailed (such as details of the crime, the time of day, the weather, the occasion) or do you prefer to "let that come out as the case evolves"?

2.2 As illustrated in Figure 2-2, you will have to resist the temptation to "learn everything" about a subject in the first case. For example, the full course in Physics may be about particle mechanics; you should focus primarily on those parts of particles mechanics that are important to the case. You need to have confidence that the other cases will give you an opportunity to learn the rest of the Physics. Think about how you are going to resist the temptation to try to learn everything. Write out your ideas and discuss them with a classmate.

2.3 A variation on the Case of the Dinged Stop Sign is given by Kardos (1971) "To Find a Bullet."

2.4 What criteria might you (and your group) use to help you limit the amount of new knowledge you try to bring to each case?

2.5 What opportunities does PBL offer to you? Use Table 1-6 as a guide.

3 *Problem solving skills*

It Just Happens:

"Problem solving? Yes, I'm pretty good at problem solving. Otherwise, I wouldn't have succeeded in school as well as I have," remarked Andy.

"How do you solve problems so successfully?" asked Annette.

"I don't know. I guess I just read the problem over carefully and work my way through it."

"That doesn't work for me", explained Jen. "But, then again, it just happens. I just solve problems. But I can't describe how I do it."

Jason suggested, "If we are going to work together in **problem-based** learning, the problem is given first. Our skill in being able to talk to each other about how we solve problems is going to be important. Let's each describe how you solve problems."

Problem solving is something we do automatically. We just do it. Rarely, are we asked to describe how and why we do it. Rarely do we see the different approaches others use. Nor do we appreciate that what might work for one, will not work for another. Here, we are **not** talking about your ability to solve problem; rather we are talking about your ability to *describe the problem-solving processes you use*.

For this situation, what do you know already?

Perhaps you already are skilled in describing your problem-solving processes. Perhaps you have had extensive experience talking aloud about the process of problem solving. If you know all of the issues and details for this situation already, skip to the next Chapter.

For this situation, what are the issues?

Some of the component skills that are used when we "problem solve" are given in Figure 3-1. Some of the issues, for the processes of solving problems, are:

1. Have confidence in your skill at problem solving.

2. Be able to describe what educational and cognitive psychologists know about how we use our minds and attitudes to solve problems effectively and efficiently.

3. Be aware of your thought processes and be able to describe them to others.

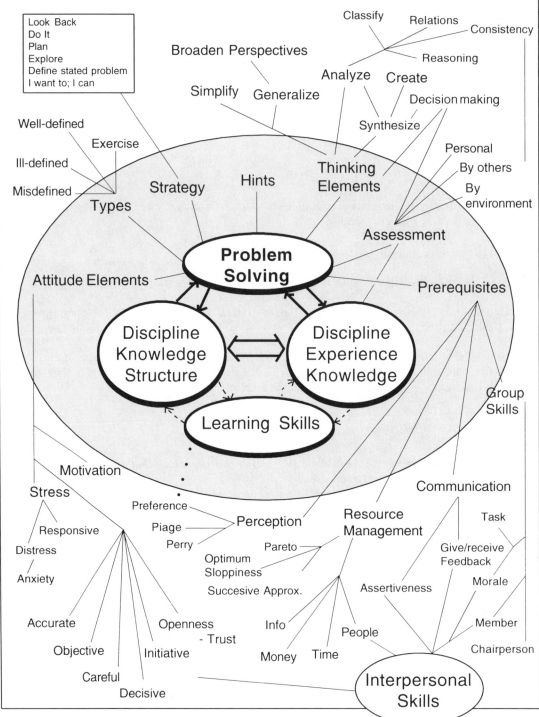

Figure 3-1 Skills that are used in "problem solving"

4. Be able to identify issues, set goals and define problems well.

5. Be organized and systematic with frequent monitoring of what you are doing.

6. Be creative, to explore many different options and issues and to try out many different strategies.

7. Identify criteria and use these to prioritize and make decisions.

8. Access and use knowledge astutely.

Each of these issues is considered in turn. You may wish to go directly to the section that answers your needs.

3.1. Have Confidence; "I want to and I can!"

Having confidence in your ability to solve problems and being willing to tackle challenging problems are, in my opinion, of critical importance. Unfortunately, most do not have that confidence. Here is what research has found. Table 3-1 gives

Table 3-1 Confidence in problem solving ability as measured by Heppner's PSI

Component in the PSI	Average	Std. dev.	Average	Std. Dev.
College students across disciplines	sophomore (N = 100)		senior (N = 43)	
Problem solving confidence	26.2	8.8	22.9	6.1
Approach avoidance	44.2	12.2	40.7	10.9
Personal control	17.5	4.8	17.0	5.5
Total PSI	87.9	22.2	80.7	19.2
Engineering students	sophomore (N = 256)		seniors (N = 32)	
Problem solving confidence	27.3	6.8	25.8	7.1
Approach avoidance	47.6	10.6	47.1	9.3
Personal control	17.4	5.2	17.6	4.3
Total PSI	91.3	18.5	90.4	16.3
Engineering students receiving training	sophomore (N = 238)		seniors (N = 202)	
Problem solving confidence	27.6	6.7	20.9	4.6
Approach avoidance	47.9	10.8	36.9	8.2
Personal control	17.6	5.2	13.2	4.0
Total PSI	92.0	18.6	71.0	14.0

the results of participants response to Heppner's PSI inventory (Heppner, 1986). This is a validated measure of three components:

- Problem solving confidence: a sense of confidence in one's ability to solve problems.

- Avoidance: willingness to engage in trying to solve difficult problems.

- Control: this is similar to Rotter's locus of control and is a measure of one's feeling of being in control of a situation (Rotter, 1966).

For all three measures, low values mean very confident, willing to engage in solving difficult problems and being in control; high values, not confident, avoiding challenging problems and a sense of not being in control. The lowest numerical value is 32; the highest, 192. (Heppner and Petersen, 1982; Heppner, 1986). Heppner's normative data for college students across academic disciplines is that students gain little confidence in their problem solving ability over the four year college program with an average of 87.9 coming into their sophomore year and 80.7 leaving their senior year for an improvement of 0.32 standard deviations. Our data for engineering students show that they enter their sophomore year with less confidence than their United States counterparts and graduate with negligible gain in confidence. Yet throughout the program the students used textbooks with many worked examples, they worked well over 2500 homework assignments and open-ended problems and they observed instructors demonstrating how they solved problems. These results of "little, to no, change in confidence in problem solving because of the fours year college experience" is confirmed by other studies (Rush et al. 1985 and 1990).

On the other hand, after 120 h of explicit workshop training, students changed from an entry value of 92 to a graduating value of 71 or an improvement of 1.13 standard deviations. During those workshops, the issues addressed were the eight highlighted in this Chapter (Woods et al., 1994).

Reflect on these issues, try to obtain feedback about how you do the tasks and monitor your progress.

3.2. Know the Problem-solving Process.

What does your mind do when you solve problems? Cognitive science tells us the following key ideas:

1. The problem solved is "our internal mental image of the problem". Figure 3-2 shows two people solving a problem involving hunters. Joe is solving the problem "as he sees it"; Janice, "as she sees it."

2. The manipulation of ideas and the actual mental problem-solving process is done in *very cramped quarters*. The section of our brain is called, by psychologists, Short Term Memory (STM). This working part of the brain can hold somewhere between 4 and 9 chunks of information at a time; more than that, it just "forgets". Contrast this with Long Term Memory (LTM). This is a vast storehouse of knowledge and experience that is called into use in STM when it is needed. The key finding is that we must become very skilled at selecting and using the information we actually work with in STM during the process of problem solving. Indeed, we write things down. We make charts and diagrams. We create clusters, or chunks, of information so that the space limitations of STM do not impede our problem-solving processes.

3. Problem solving is a complex interaction between the subject knowledge we have in LTM and the processes used to monitor, select, retrieve and work with in crowded STM. In this Chapter we focus on the processes and call these "problem solving".

4. Contrast "problem solving" with "exercise solving". In exercise solving, we recall and apply past routines that we used successfully for similar problems. Typically, we work forwards. That is, we know the given or

starting information, make connections between the given information, our past experience and the goal, and piece these together as we work forwards to the goal. In problem solving, we initially are unsure as to how to proceed and are unsure about the connection between the given data and the goal. Typically, we work backwards. We start at the goal and work back to search for connections between the goal and the given information. Norman (1984) suggests that expert clinical MDs encounter 95% exercises.

If you need to learn more about these characteristics and their implications, Woods (1988, and 1994a) provides more details.

In addition to the research from cognitive science, successful problem solvers apply five principles as they work through the process of solving problems. These five principles are:

- The "law of optimum sloppiness" which says that for any situation, there is an optimum amount of sloppiness that we can use to resolve the situation. The corollary is "that there are occasions when we must be sloppy and imprecise in our approach; there are times when we must be precise. We should only be as complicated as the situation warrants". In PBL, we apply this by continually asking "What do we **need** to know in this problem?" Do we have the resources to meet those needs? If not, how can we adjust our needs?" In PBL, we must take the time to astutely identify the "needs" and "key issues" in the problem that are worthy of study *for the resources we have available.*

- The "principle of successive approximation or successive development" says that we should start simply and get an idea for the order-of-magnitude of the answer at the beginning. We solve the problem with gross approximations first. Then if the answer seems reasonable, we solve it with more accurate information, and we invest more resources to improve the accuracy of the answer. So we progress. Keep It Simple at the Start! In the context of PBL, this is a critical overall principle. As described in Chapter 2, one's tendency is to "try to learn everything in a subject". PBL is designed to build up your knowledge successively across a wide range of

Figure 3-2 The mental images of two problem solvers when they encounter the problem "Hunters went into the woods..."

topics and in the context of a problem to be solved. Focus on not what you "want" to learn; focus first on what you **need** to learn and on what issues **need** to be addressed to solve the problem.

- Prioritize by applying "the Pareto principle" or the "80/20 rule". This principle suggests that 80% of the benefit or results can be achieved with 20% of the effort. Thus, 80% of the sales comes from 20% of the customers; 80% of the telephone calls come from 20% of the callers. The corollary is that 80% of the damage is results from 20% of the causes. Thus, 80% of the maintenance is caused by 20% of the causes. In PBL, Pareto's principle suggests that for any problem 80% of the problem can be solved by identifying the correct 20% of the issues. Focus on identifying those key issues.

- The "12/1 rule for satisfaction". From the literature on customer satisfaction, researchers found that 12 positive experiences are needed to overcome 1 negative experience (Seymour, 1992). We might extend this to learning via PBL or learning of the skills related to it (like problem solving skills). If you have had 1 negative experience in solving problems, you will want to encounter 12 successful experiences to overcome that negative experience.

- the "85/15 rule for the source of the problem": 85% of problems occur because of the rules and regulations; 15% of the problems are because of the people (Seymour, 1992). So what? In the context of PBL, scrutinize the issues and ensure that, where appropriate to the case or problem, that issues related to rules and regulations are considered. Ensure that the ground-rules you establish, as to how you will function in the PBL program, do not impede your progress.

In summary, much is known about the processes we use and the principles we apply when we solve problems. Reflect and apply these.

3.3 Become Aware of Your Problem-solving Processes.

To gain confidence and to improve our skills, we need to be able to describe what goes on in our mind as we solve problems. We can then compare those processes with those of successful problem solvers; discard the bad habits and polish and develop those that promote success. You could develop the required awareness by

- using Talk Aloud Pairs Problem Solving (in which one person plays the role of listener, and one, the talker/problem solver). For more see Woods (1984, 1994a), MPS Unit 1 and Whimbey and Lochhead (1982).

- talking into a tape recorder and then critiquing the result.

3.4 Identify Issues and Define Problems Carefully

Unsuccessful problem solvers tend to spend most of their time *doing* something whereas successful problem solvers spend most of their time deciding **what** to do. In general, spend about half your time allotted to solving a problem to **defining** the goal; defining the problem. This task is challenging. Indeed, it is so challenging that research has suggested that it be divided into the three separate stages illustrated in Figure 3-3. The different stages are:

Engage: "I Want to & I Can"

We encounter a situation where there seems to be a problem. We read a given problem statement (like a starting Problem in PBL or like an exercise in this book). We listen to a tutor verbally describe a situation that needs to be resolved, a decision that needs to be made. We observe something. We "engage" in reading, listening, seeing, hearing about the situation and the "problem". Larkin (1980) found that successful problem solvers spent two to three times longer reading an initial problem statement than did unsuccessful problem solvers.

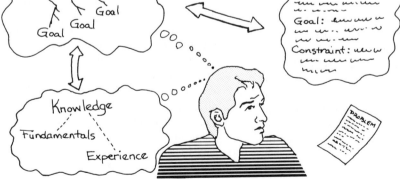

Figure 3-3 Three stages to "defining problems"

Spend the time carefully reading the problem statement, engaging in learning about the situation that poses the problem. Read all of the information that we are given. When we complete this, our main task is to motivate ourselves to continue; we need to want to solve it. We should also have confidence that we can solve it; that we can solve it. We need to overcome our panic. This stage is predominantly mental preparation before we dive into the details of trying to solve it. Attempt to capture the flavour of this stage by saying aloud, "I want to & I can". This is one third of the task of "defining the problem."

Define the stated problem

The next part of "defining the problem" is to understand, "What does the problem statement say?" Do we understand all of the words? Our objective is to *understand the problem as it is given to us*. We analyze and classify the information into the parts. Given problem statements usually include:

a. The stated objective, goal, thing to solve, decision to make, unknown to quantify, value to determine, option to select, feature to identify. This is "what we are asked to do". For example, "Find the force". Some PBL problem statements do **not** include a goal statement. A situation is described.

b. The situation, conditions or context. What are the inputs? what is the system? what is included and what is excluded? what is known? what is the situation? For example, "Jeremy Bridgewood, an 11 year old boy, fell from a bridge 10 metres into a rocky creek bed. He was helped out of the water and taken to the nearest hospital. He talked somewhat en route. But on examination at the hospital, no verbal response was elicited." (reprinted courtesy of McMaster University Medical School, copyright 1992) In this example, we have many questions: Who helped him out of the water? How much water was there in the creek? Was he under the water? How long did it take to get to the hospital? Put those

questions on reserve right now. Focus on the given situation and given information.
- an 11 year old boy;
- fell 10 metres into a rocky creek bed;
- during the period of time immediately after the fall, he talked (details unknown);
- later (at the hospital) no verbal response elicited.

c. The constraints: on the inputs, on the solution and on the process we can use. For example, "You have three weeks to consider this case."

d. The criteria by which we will judge an acceptable answer. For example, "Your solution must satisfy your initial criteria; the evidence must substantiate your hypothesis." Often "constraints" become "criteria". For example, if the constraint is that we must complete the task in 20 min., then a "criterion" for successfully reaching our goal is, "Did we complete the task in 20 min?" The constraint becomes a criterion.

Some optional activities, during this stage, might include drawing a picture, selecting some nomenclature, considering the inferred constraints and criteria, translating the problem statement into a visual format, an equation or symbolic format or a verbal format. The word "optional" is included because, although most people do this stage about the same way, some prefer to transform it into a visual picture or into an equation "because they can think better in those terms." They prefer to do this transformation before they identify the goal, or list the inputs/situation, or identify the constraints and criteria. That's OK. Use your preference. Nevertheless, the focus is **not** on solving the problem, **not** on understanding what the problem really is, **not** on creating the internal image of the problem. It is on classifying the given information into different categories: the goal, the givens, the constraints and the criteria. This is the second part of the task of "defining the problem." We monitor this stage by asking such questions as, "Have all of the conditions of the problem been noted?" "Has the stated goal been stated correctly?"

Explore

This stage is probably the most underrated, most challenging and least understood stage of all the stages. Indeed, it was only in the 1970's that this step was clearly identified as a separate step by the research of Schoenfeld (1979) and our work Woods et al. (1975). In this step we play around with the problem statement and with our background subject knowledge and experience in solving problems. We try to discover what the "real" problem is. We try to recast it into our understanding of the situation. At this stage we make no commitments toward a solution or toward an answer. We search for important links. We try to discover reasonable assumptions; to identify what can be left out and what must be considered. Exploring combines such skills as creating, analyzing, generalizing, simplifying, translating, seeing many different points-of-view, and broadening and narrowing our view. The activities are complex and differ greatly from individual to individual.

While we are creating our internal image we:

a. *Create our personal, rich mental image of the situation.* We recall from memory ideas related to the stated goal, the context and all the features that seem pertinent both inside and outside of the context. We elaborate. Gradually we will settle in on "our best mental representation of the problem."

b. *Zero-in on the **real** goal.* We do this by placing the "problem statement" in the context of our mental image of the situation. We play around with the stated goal and explore whether that really is the right goal. We ask, "Is this really the goal that is the *most worthwhile for us to address*?" For example, in the case of Jeremy Bridgewood, is the real goal to keep him alive? Is this a life-threatening incident? At the other extreme, one might suggest that the real goal should be to prevent other kids from falling off the bridge. We revise and adjust our image. Gradually we will settle in on "the real goal."

c. *Highlight the critical features of the situation.* Recall that problem solving is finding the best answer "subject to the constraints". The constraints are critical features that determine the degree of complexity, the amount of information and the amount of resources available. We usually do this by making the problem as simple as possible. We make all kinds of "simplifying assumptions". We remove the constraints. We ask "What if? what if? what if?" We solve simple approximations to see what kind of answers we get. We guess. We make mistakes. Keep it simple at the start! We probe to see what is really important in this particular problem. Gradually we will settle in on a range of assumptions about the context.

d. *Guestimate an answer.*

e. *Create a series of options or hypotheses on how to achieve the goal*; on how to solve the problem. We play around with various ways we might achieve the goal. We redefine our mental image of the situation, redefine the real goal, and use our imagination to think of many options. This may give us a revised mental image, a revised "real" goal and some idea as to how we might "solve the problem". This process evolves into the "Plan" stage where we begin to set out concrete suggestions as to what we will do.

The monitoring questions we use during this stage include: "What is the simplest view? What other views or perspectives might be pertinent? What am I really trying to accomplish? Have I included all the pertinent issues? When I solve this, so what? What is the potential usefulness of each proposed idea? When a mistake is made, ask 'what did I learn from this?' Am I keeping all my options open? Am I ready to leave this stage for the time being?"

In summary, defining the real problem is an extremely challenging task. If we do it wrong, we solve the wrong problem. We cannot see the result of the mental processing, because each of us has created out own mental image of the situation. It is that mental image that each of us solves. We all do the task differently. The key message is to

> take time to do the task well and communicate with each other to get some idea of the mental image of others.

3.5 Be Organized, Systematic and Monitor

Use a strategy. An example is Polya's four-step strategy of "Define, Plan, Do it and Look back". Most have developed their own strategy. However, for group problem solving, a commonly accepted strategy is a prerequisite to effective communication. Based on a survey of over 60 published strategies, the research implications summarized in Section 3.1, and the 3-stage model of "defining a problem" (given in Section 3.4) we recommend the use of the MPS 6-stage strategy summarized in Figure 3-4. This representation shows the stages as rooms about a central hall. The central hall gives access to any of the stages. Beside each stage are listed the cognitive or thinking skills used and the attitudes required. The former are shown in arabic letters; the attitudes, in *italics.* Thus, during the Engage, I want to and I can stage, the cognitive skills used are "read and listen". The attitudes needed are "anxiety, stress management, motivation, confidence, risk, unafraid of making a mistake and monitor".

The other 3-stages, in addition to the 3-stages for "defining the problem," are Plan, Do it and Look back. Here are some details.

Plan

The Exploration stage gives us an overview of what the problem is and of how we are going to solve it. The separation line between Explore and Plan is often very blurred. This Explore stage evolves into the Plan stage when we get down to the business of mapping out the subproblems and the steps to be taken; of listing the data to be collected; of noting the hypotheses to be tested. Usually we select plans from among such different tactics as working backwards, systematic trial-and-error, break it into subproblems, prove contradiction or contrapositive, or make inferences (Wickelgren, 1974; Stonewater, 1976; Solow, 1982). The monitoring questions we use during this stage might be, "What is the overall, organized plan? Is this plan well structured? Is the plan relevant? How can I assess the quality of the plan? How can I monitor progress?"

Do It

Methodically and systematically we carry out the plan. We do it.

Look Back

This evaluation stage is usually not done very well, if it is done at all. Yet, this stage holds the greatest potential for the acknowledgement of success and for improving our ability to solve problems. We should manage of delight at having successfully completed the task and take time to look back. We should check that our answer is reasonable and error-free, and that our answer satisfies the criteria and the goal. We should look at the process we used to solve the problem and explore what we learned about problem solving. We might identify "experience factors" that we encountered and that will be useful in the future. Above all, we should create other problems that would be solved using the same subject fundamentals. In this way we prepare ourselves and anticipate their future occurrence. Other related activities could include implement, communicate and prevent the problem from reoccurring. The monitoring questions might include, "How do I terminate this stage? How might I monitor this stage?"

Transition

A transition stage exists after each of the six listed above. In Figure 3-4 this is the central corridor.

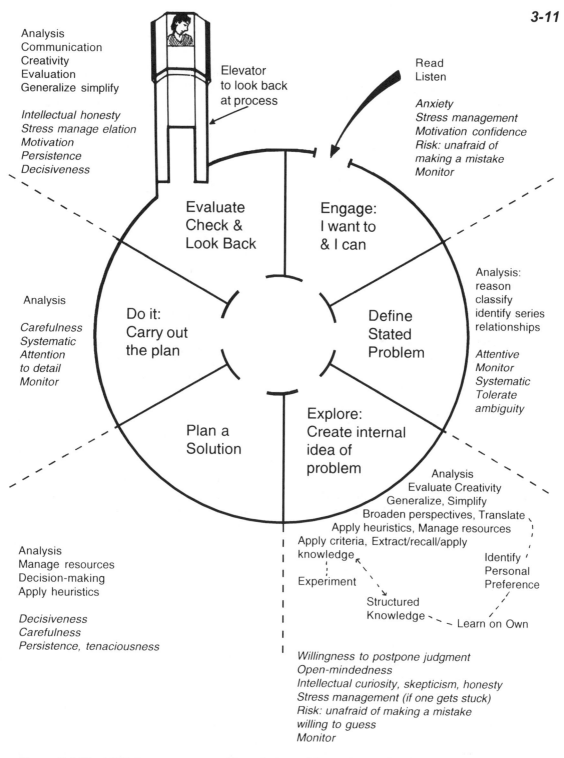

Figure 3-4 The MPS 6-stage strategy with typical cognitive and *attitudinal* skills noted for each stage

This stage is mainly a monitoring stage where we ask:

   - "Where am I in the process of obtaining a solution? How do I assess my progress?

   - How can I salvage and store valuable components from a failed avenue of attack?

   - What do I do now? What new avenue or stage should I follow? How does what I have just done affect my decision?

      -What do I anticipate the outcomes to be from this next stage?"

Three features of this strategy are noteworthy.

1. The 6-stages are **not** shown serially because, in reality, we do not use them serially. We bounce back and forth among the stages. We engage, then define, then engage, then explore then, perhaps, go back to engage.

2. Unlike many published strategies, the words "idea finding" or "create options" or "analyze" are not used in any of the titles of the stages. This is because we use such thinking skills as creativity and analysis *whenever we need to*. We do not restrict their use to one particular stage. Some of the attitudes and thinking skills that are needed in different stages are illustrated in Figure 3-4.

3. We may interrupt the whole process and start to apply the whole 6-stage strategy to a subproblem. Thus, the 6-stage strategy can be "nested" and used many different times in solving one particular problem. For example, if the clock strikes 13, then the 6-stage strategy is applied once to solve the overall process of "fixing it". In addition, the strategy is applied three more times, once for each of three subproblems: to identify the fault, to correct it and to prevent it from happening again. Thus, the 6-stage strategy would be applied once overall and "nested" and applied to each of the three subproblems. Figure 3-5 is another illustration of "nesting". In this illustration the overall problem facing the pharmacist is to "solve the patient's

problem". A pharmacist often uses the following steps.

Step 1, Identify issues associated with the patient's drug therapy. Gather data.

Step 2, Identify the real drug-related problem you are going to solve for this patient. What's the real problem?

Step 3, What are the optimal therapeutic outcomes for each of the problems?

Step 4, What are the therapeutic alternatives?
    4b, What are the best options?
    4c, Select the best therapeutic action.
    4d, Select the best monitoring program.

Step 5, Pharmacist's drug recommendation and individualization. What drug regimen should be instituted? What changes to existing therapy? What specific dose, dose formulation, regimen and duration?

Step 6, Intervention: prescribe the drugs and give instructions.

Step 7, Therapeutic drug monitoring. How do I ensure that the desired is happening, that the undesired is minimized and with what frequency do I check?

At first glance, this strategy seems to be completely different from the MPS 6-stage strategy. Then, we realize that many of these steps require the solution to a subproblem. We apply the full strategy to solve each subproblem. In this example, most of the mental action occurs between the initial encounter with the patient (Stage 1 in the MPS 6-stage) and the delivery of the drug and the instructions (the "Do it", Stage 6, in the MPS 6-stage). However, the intervening steps of identifying the real problem, of exploring outcomes, and of selecting the options, actions and the monitoring are subproblems on their own. Thus, in Figure 3-5, these are shown as complete, nested applications of the overall 6-stage strategy. In summary, we may use the same strategy many times in solving "one problem".

The three main advantages of using such as strategy as the MPS 6-stage are 1) that having a strategy helps us overcome the initial panic that wells up when we face a tough problem and 2) the strategy helps us to work systematically. Most of all, identifying stages in the process reminds us to

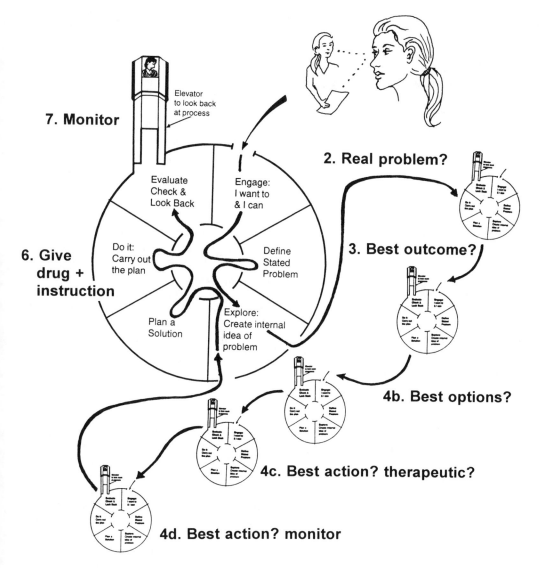

7. Monitor

Elevator to look back at process

6. Give drug + instruction

Evaluate Check & Look Back

Engage: I want to & I can

Do it: Carry out the plan

Define Stated Problem

Plan a Solution

Explore: Create internal idea of problem

2. Real problem?

3. Best outcome?

4b. Best options?

4c. Best action? therapeutic?

4d. Best action? monitor

Figure 3-5 Nested strategies shows multiple application of the same MPS 6-stage strategy in the solution of one problem

monitor our thought processes. In monitoring, we do such things as:

- Assess the potential use of each idea before we apply it: "When I calculate this, then...".

- Assess whether a subtask is complete: "Have I defined the problem?".
- Assess what we learn from mistakes.
- Monitor at least once per minute: "Why am I doing this?", or "What have I done so far?"

More details about monitoring were given above for each of the 6-stages.

As you talk aloud, learn to use words and phrases that show you are monitoring and assessing your processes. If you need more information about strategies and monitoring, the MPS Problem Solving Program that complements this book provides enrichment in MPS **4**.

3.6 Enrich your Creativity

Whereas being systematic tends to yield linear sequences of ideas, we need to be flexible and be able to think laterally. Instead of thinking up 5 issues, we should be skilled at generating 50 issues in five minutes. The popular term is "brainstorming". The principles are that we:

- Defer criticism and judgement of ideas.
- Encourage building on ideas from others.
- Express ideas succinctly. No elaboration is required as to how something might work.
- Repetition of ideas is OK.
- Use triggers to restart a flow of ideas. Some triggers are listed in Table 3-2.

- Use checklists, like SCAMPER.
- Suggest crazy ideas.
- Reverse ideas.
- Juxtapose random words.
- Remove boundary.

Table 3-2 Some triggers for brainstorming

- Learn to cope positively with those silences and negative feelings that usually occur when you think you have run out of ideas.
- Announce, "Let's brainstorm!" and then ensure that all are familiar with ground rules. Table 3-3 gives a checklist that might be used to monitor the progress of each brainstorming session.

If you want more about creativity, read van Gundy (1981), de Bono (1972), Isaksen and Treffinger (1985), Woods (1994b) or MPS Unit **7** in the McMaster Problem Solving program that complements this book.

3.7 Set Criteria and Make Decisions

We make better decisions if we apply explicit, measurable criteria. Criteria are defined as the measure we use to choose or decide on merit. For example, to choose the tallest person the *criterion* is "height". To choose the cheapest radio, the *criterion* is "money". To select the best location for an office building, the *criteria* might include rent, aesthetics, commuting distance for the employees, the prestige of the neighbourhood, and local facilities available. In this example, many criteria are listed but not expressed in measurable terms. The first requirement is that we must have criteria to make a decision. The second requirement is that those criteria should be expressed in terms that can be measured. Hence, the "commuting distance for employees" might, be measured as a "commuting time of less than 30 min." A third characteristic of criteria is that there are three types of criteria: must, want and minimize adverse circumstances. "Must" criteria **must** be satisfied. If they are not, then the option is thrown out. In the example in Table 3-4, five criteria were "must" criteria and the three options all satisfied these criteria. These are Yes-No criteria in that the option is acceptable only if the criteria is satisfied. Once the "must" criteria are satisfied, we then consider the characteristics we **want**. "Want" criteria are those things we prefer would occur. In the example in Table 3-4, ten criteria are want criteria. We pick the options that have the highest ratings for the "want" criteria. To obtain ratings, we assign a relative "weighting" as to the importance of each want criterion. For example, travel time is assigned a weighting of 10. Then, independent of the weighting, each option is rated on a scale from 0 to 10 for each "want" criteria. For example, option Ancaster is assigned a rating of "8" for the want criteria of "time for others to travel to work"; a rating of "10" for its decor, and a rating of "7" for its parking. To put this all together, the weighting for each want criterion is multiplied by the rating for each option to get a total for each criterion for each option. These are totalled to give 596 for Ancaster etc. Thus, based on all the **must** criteria being satisfied, and based on the largest total of the **want** criteria, Ancaster should be the location of the new office. The third criterion is to "minimize adverse circumstances". Since some adverse or negative events could occur in the future, we want to account for this possibility as a criterion. For example, the office complex could be sold to a new owner, a new road could be put in or a new school built. For any decision, brainstorm possible negative events that could happen, estimate the probability or

"likelihood" that they occur and guess the "seriousness" because it occurs. Assign a number from 0 to 10 for each,; then multiply the likelihood by the seriousness. Hopefully, the attractive option will also have the least total of the adverse effects. Thus, we make decisions based on measurable criteria; satisfy the **must** criteria, get the best of the **want** criteria and have the minimum of the adverse effects. Other approaches to decision-making are used (Kepner and Tregoe, 1976; Janis and Mann, 1977 and Arnold, 1978 and 1992) but they all use measurable criteria.

Table 3-3 Monitoring checklist for brainstorming

Number of Ideas generated _____ Activity or problem: _____

In the session: rate the following out of 10:

How much elaboration?
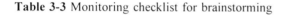
| 0 | 2 | 4 | 6 | 8 | 10 |
Extensive — None, all succinct ideas

How much criticism?
| 0 | 2 | 4 | 6 | 8 | 10 |
Extensive — None

How many silences?
| 0 | 2 | 4 | 6 | 8 | 10 |
Extensive — Few

Triggers used? No ☐   Yes ☐ give name(s)

craziest   boundary   personal   function juxtaposition checklist morph
book title replacement reverse   senses   fishbone   wave   other

Strengths   Areas to work on
_____   _____
_____   _____
_____
_____   from D.R. Woods, "How to Gain the Most from PBL", 1994
_____

| Decision or results to be achieved (reword action statement into results expected) | To obtain the best office space to meet our needs | | | | | | | | Action? (Results) | |

		Option Ancaster			Option Burlington			Option Stay Where We Are		
Constraint/Must	Less than 30 min.	15mins.			18mins.			13mins.		
	Max. $20,000/a	$15,483			$15,900			$13,070		
	Max. 3 year lease	2 yr.			3 yr.			2 yr.		
	Min. 1850 ft.²	1950 ft.²			2200 ft.²			2030 ft.²		
	Occupancy Jan. 1	Yes			Yes			Yes		

	Wt.		Rate			Rate			Rate	
Criteria & Positive Effects Min. travel										
Time for others	10	15mins.	8	80	10mins.	10	100	15mins.	8	80
Max. use space	10	Very good	9	90	Excellent	10	100	Not well laid out	5	50
Decor	9	Beautiful	10	90	Good potential	6	54	Not good	2	18
Min. time to 403	9	2nd best	7	63	Best	10	90	Worst	4	36
Min. rental	9		8	72		7	63	Best	10	90
2 yr. lease	8	Yes	10	80	No	0	0	Yes	10	80
Quiet	8	Very quiet	10	80	Yes, but kids	6	48	Noisy	2	16
Separate conference	5	No, but office	4	20	Yes, if modify	8	40	Yes	10	50
Parking	3	Good	7	21	Plenty	10	30	Crowded	5	15
TOTAL Maximum				596			525			435

Adverse & Negative Effects Create adverse consequences for each option. For each consequence estimate L: likelihood of happening (0 to 10) and the S: impact or seriousness if it does (0 to 10) Multiply L x S	L	S	LxS		L	S	LxS		L	S	LxS
New owner	2	3	6		New owner	3	4	12				
New traffic route	1	8	8		New school	4	4	16				
TOTAL Minimum			14				28					

Table 3-4 Making decisions: an example

effects. Other approaches to decision-making are used (Kepner and Tregoe, 1976; Janis and Mann, 1977 and Arnold, 1978 and 1992) but they all use measurable criteria.

Arnold (1978) suggests the AAP approach for creating criteria. In this approach we ask, "What do I want to Achieve, Avoid and Preserve?" through this decision.

In summary, some criteria we **must** satisfy; others, we **want** to satisfy. Table 3-4 gives a convenient worksheet (and example) of criteria and a decision. If you need to know more about decision-making and criteria, then my favourite resources are Kepner and Tregoe (1976), Janis and Mann (1977) and Arnold (1978 and 1992). The companion McMaster Problem Solving program addresses these skills in MPS **23** and **24** and Woods (1994b).

3.8 Make Astute Use of Knowledge

We solve problems by bringing to bear the appropriate knowledge. But what is appropriate? How skilled are you in the process? In problem solving **and** in PBL, four important uses of knowledge are as follows. We need to

- Identify the key information about the problem situation so as to define the real problem. Most "textbook" problems you encountered in the past gave you all the information you needed to solve the problem. Not too much. Not too little. Just the right amount. (Indeed, quickly you may have realized that you can play around with the given information to discover what "formula" or "equation" *used up* all the given information.) In solving *real-world* problems, - and in learning via PBL - we have to find out what the problem really is. We elaborate on the given information based on our past experience. We ask questions, seek clarification, probe assumptions, raise issues, see the situation from a variety of points-of-view. Table 3-5 lists some of these viewpoints. We need skill in doing this.

- Recall and assess which past subject knowledge and experience is pertinent. The key words are **assess** and **pertinent**. Even in solving "textbook" problems, this may not be a trivial task. Larkin (1976) found some surprising results in her research of freshman students solving Physics problems. The unsuccessful problem solvers tried to apply *more* subject knowledge than did the

successful problems solvers. It was not the apparent "lack of knowledge" that made them unsuccessful. Rather, they pulled out everything they thought might be pertinent and tried it. This is illustrated, to some extent, in Figure 3-6. Here, an unsuccessful student working on a problem in electrical circuits tries Equation 5, then Equation 7, then Equations 8 and 9 hoping that some of these might eventually work. Contrast this with the successful problem solver working on a problem of a rotating falling disk. The successful problem solver rapidly selected "pointers" that showed a direct and rapid connection with fundamental principles and methods. In summary, recalling past, pertinent subject knowledge is not a trivial task.

- Identify and learn new subject knowledge. (The issues related to this are described in Chapter 6.)

- Assess the value of the knowledge. We critically appraise the information we have and gather information that really "tests" and clarifies the hypotheses and issues. Elstein et al. (1978) and Woods (1993) review the challenges of doing this in the area of clinical problem solving and trouble shooting, respectively.

The astute use of knowledge draws on skill in asking probing questions, resolving conflicting evidence, recalling appropriate information based on fundamentals, continually cross-checking points-of-view with the data to check for consistency, critically appraising information and assessing the quality of the data available.

3.9 The Role of the Tutor

In any PBL program, the role of the tutor should be clarified so that all are aware of the expectations one has of each other. If the tutor is part of your group, Wilkerson (1994) reports that you will probably look to the tutor to:

Table 3-5 Triggers for "points-of-view" and "issues"

Purpose or context:	Trigger questions or perspectives to consider:	Example or elaboration
broaden viewpoint; put a problem in context:	Ask "Why?" "Why?" "Why?" until reach "happiness and bliss"	How might I determine the best price? **why**? so I don't feel cheated? How might I keep from feeling cheated? **why**? so that I have I good self image. How might I have a good self image? **why**? so that I ..
sharpen perspectives:	Ask "What's stopping you?"	How might I determine the best price? **WSY**? I'm afraid to ask.
prioritize issues:	Guess the solution; and then work backwards.	When we have many competing issues, trying to visualize the final product and the key components in that product may help prioritize the issues.
completeness, identifying the "system":	5Ws & H; IS and IS NOT; on and by	What is in the system, what is not? what is being done **on** me? what is being done **by** me? who is in the system, who is not? what on me? what is being done by me?
PBL in medical school	biological perspective: (structure, function and pharmacology) behavioral perspective: population perspective:	
PBL in technology	scientific underpinnings: technological: operability and maintainability: financial: financial attractiveness: safety: ethical and legal: environmental: value to society:	
PBL in history	social: cultural/intellectual: political: diplomatic economic: environmental: psychological:	

a. Unsuccessful problem-solver's script for a circuit problem

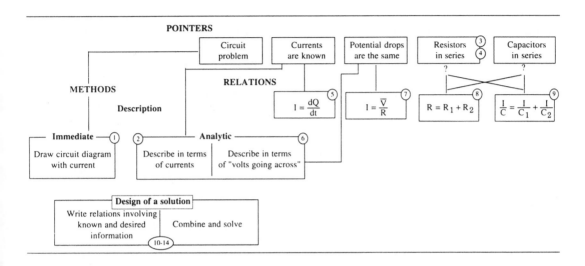

b. Successful problem-solver's script for a falling-disk problem.

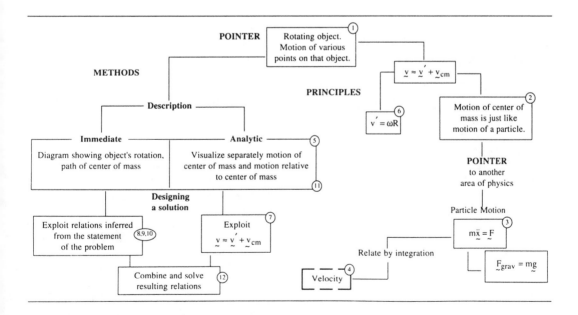

Figure 3-6 Problem solver's processing of knowledge

- Ask probing questions and question you to ensure that you understand what you are doingand why you are taking this particular approach to solve the problem.

- If you give ideas, the tutor will ask you to reflect on those ideas and justify why the information is consistent with the evidence.

However, if the tutor continually supplies these skills, then how do you develop them for yourself? These are valued skills to possess!

If the tutor does not supply them, or you have a group empowered to function without a tutor, how do you ensure that **you** provide the skills? Clarify this with your group.

For individuals working on PBL and for those who wish to develop their own problem solving skills, you should assume this responsibility of continually monitoring, clarifying and justifying the approach you are taking in solving the problem.

The basic idea for the development of any skill is:

If you value the skill, then make the skill a desired outcome!

To understand the outcome, express the outcome as an observable goal that has measurable criteria!

To show that the outcome has been achieved, explore how to present evidence of accomplishment!

To internalize the skill, reflect and self assess and use it in different contexts!

Regardless of the variation in approach to PBL, you should clarify the role of the tutor in helping you with your problem solving approaches.

3.10 Summary and How to Monitor Progress

Problem-based learning starts with a *problem*. You need to be confident in and skilled at problem solving to progress effectively and efficiently. Research has shown that confidence and skills are developed if you become aware of your problem-solving processes, reflect and monitor what you do, are systematic, are skilled at seeing things from different perspectives and can create many different ideas, if you take time to deliberately and carefully define the problem and if you use measurable criteria in making decisions.

Table 3-6 gives a checklist you can use to monitor your problem solving approaches.

3.11 References

Arnold, J.D (1978) "Make up your mind!" Amacom, 135 West 50th St., New York, NY.

Arnold, J.D. (1992) "The Complete Problem Solver," J. Wiley and Sons, New York, NY.

de Bono, E., (1972) "PO: Beyond Yes and No," Penguin Books, Harmondsworth, UK.

Elstein, A.S., L.S. Shulman, S.A. Sprafka (1978) "Medical Problem Solving: an analysis of clinical reasoning," Harvard University Press, Cambridge, MA.

Heppner, P.P. and C.H. Petersen (1982) "The Development and Implications of a Personal Problem-solving Inventory," J. Counselling Psychology, **29**, 1, 66-75.

Heppner, P.P. (1986) "The PSI Manual," 210 McAlester Hall, University of Missouri-Columbia, Columbia, MO 65211.

Isaksen, S.G., and D.J. Treffinger (1985) "Creative Problem Solving: the basic course," Bearly Ltd., Buffalo, NY.

Table 3-6 Feedback about problem solving

Attribute		Assessment
Awareness	+ can describe processes, can distinguish "exercise solving" from "PS."	
	- unaware of process; it's intuitive; cannot define a framework for PS.	
Variety of PS skills	+ can apply a variety of methods and hints.	
	- knows very few techniques; attempts to use a "one-step" solution.	
Emphasis on accuracy	+ checks, double checks, rechecks; concern for accuracy.	
	- concern for speed; unwilling to check.	
Active	+ writes things down, makes lists, prioritizes, makes tables and sketches;	
	- thinks in head, can't keep track, stares at paper.	
Monitors & reflects	+ assesses continually, assesses potential of ideas & options; continually evaluates and curtails; asks "where is this getting me?"	
	- does not monitor or assess; just does something.	
Organized & systematic	+ plans, anticipates, develops and uses a systematic plan.	
	- trial & error, impulsive, jumps around; no plan.	
Flexible & sees OPV	+ keeps options open; sees different points-of-view, willing to discard.	
	- quickly becomes fixed on one or two ideas or options even when mounting evidence proves these to be untenable; unwilling to discard.	
Use of knowledge: objective & critically assesses	+ objective, learns from others, critically assesses data.	
	- fails to draw on past experience, egocentric, assumes & believes everything they are told; accepts all information without question.	
Welcomes challenge	+ identifies disequilibrium as good; welcomes change and confusion.	
	- considers confusion to be "bad."	
Time allocation	+ spends most of time in exploring, defining, planning and engage stages.	
	- spends most time doing, calculating, writing.	
Overall approach	+ based on fundamentals, underlying principles, needs & goals.	
	- searches for sample solutions & cooks to try to make them work.	
Decision-making	+ applies criteria, draws conclusions substantiated by evidence.	
	- makes a selection based on "gut" reaction.	

Strengths   Areas to work on

_____   _____

_____   _____

_____

_____

_____ from D.R. Woods "How to Gain the Most from PBL," 1994.

Janis, I.L. and L. Mann (1977) "Decision Making," The Free Press, New York, NY.

Kepner, C.H. and B.B. Tregoe (1976) "The Rational Manager," Princeton, NJ.

Larkin, J.H. (1976) "Cognitive Structures and Problem Solving Ability," Paper JL060176, Group in Science and Mathematics Education, University of California, Berkeley, CA.

Larkin, J.H. (1980) "Spatial Reasoning in Solving Physics Problems," Carnegie Mellon University, Pittsburgh, PA., personal communication.

Norman, G.R. (1984) McMaster University Medical School, Hamilton, ON. personal communication.

MPS **1** (1985) "Awareness," Department of Chemical Engineering, McMaster University, Hamilton.

MPS **4** (1985) "Strategy," Department of Chemical Engineering, McMaster University, Hamilton.

MPS **7** (1985) "Creativity," Department of Chemical Engineering, McMaster University, Hamilton.

MPS **23** (1987) "Obtaining Criteria," Department of Chemical Engineering, McMaster University, Hamilton.

MPS **24** (1985) "Decision making," Department of Chemical Engineering, McMaster University, Hamilton.

Polya, G. (1957) "How to Solve It," 2nd ed., Princeton University Press, Princeton, NJ.

Rotter, J.B. (1966) "Generalized expectancies for internal versus external control of reinforcement," Psychological Monographs, **80**, (1, Whole No. 609).

Rush, J.C., J.A. Krmpotic and F.T. Evers "Making the Match between university graduates and corporate employers" Part I, 1985; Part II, 1990, Canadian Corporate Higher Education Forum, Montreal, PQ. see also PS News **70**, 1990.

Schoenfeld, A.H. (1979) "Teaching Mathematical Problem Solving," preprint, Hamilton College, Clinton, NY.

Schoenfeld, A.H. (1985) "Mathematical Problem Solving," Academic Press, Orlando, FL.

Schoenfeld, A.H. (1983) "Episodes and Executive Decisions in Mathematical Problem Solving," in "Acquisition of Mathematics, Concepts and Processes," R. Lesh and M. Landau, ed., Academic Press, New York, NY.

Seymour, D.T. (1992) "On Q: causing quality in higher education," Ace/MacMillan, New York, NY.

Solow, D. (1982) "How to Read and Do Proofs," J. Wiley and Sons, New York, NY.

Stonewater, J. (1976) "Introduction to Reasoning and Problem Solving," notes from Michigan State University, Lansing. MI.

van Gundy, A.B., Jr. (1981) "Techniques of Structured Problem Solving," van Nostrand Reinhold Co., New York, NY.

Whimbey, A. and J. Lochhead (1982) "Problem Solving and Comprehension," 3rd ed., Franklin Institute Press, Philadelphia, PA.

Wickelgren, W.A. (1974) "How to Solve Problems," W.H. Freeman and Co., San Francisco, CA.

Wilkerson, LuAnn (1994) "Identification of Skills for the Problem-based Tutor: Student and Faculty Perspectives," seminar at McMaster University, Hamilton, ON

Woods, D.R., J.D. Wright, T.W. Hoffman, R.K. Swartman and I.D. Doig (1975) "Teaching Problem Solving Skills," Engineering Education, **66**, 3, 238-243.

Woods, D.R. (1984) "PS Corner," J. College Science Teaching, 13, 6, 467-472.

Woods, D.R. (1988) "Problem Solving," in "What Research says to the College Science Teacher: Problem Solving," D.Gabel, ed., National Science Teachers Association, Washington, DC.

Woods, D.R. (1993) "Trouble Shooting Skills," Department of Chemical Engineering, McMaster University, Hamilton, ON.

Woods, D.R., R.R. Marshall, A.N. Hrymak, C.M. Crowe and P.E. Wood (1994) "MPS Program for Teaching Problem Solving Skills," Department of Chemical Engineering, McMaster University, Hamilton

Woods, D.R. (1994a) "The MPS Strategy Book" Department of Chemical Engineering, McMaster University, Hamilton.

Woods, D.R. (1994b) "The MPS Idea Book," Department of Chemical Engineering, McMaster University, Hamilton.

3.12 Exercises

3.1 The first of eight tasks described in Chapter 2 is "Explore the problem, create hypotheses, identify issues". This is usually the most challenging task you will encounter early in a PBL program. For some, a tutor will be available to develop your skill in "exploring and seeing the problem statement" from many different viewpoints. In programs with 1 tutor for more than 5 students, you will need to develop this skill mainly on your own. Regardless of your access to a tutor, this ability to identify a rich set of issues for any problem is a skill you should nurture. One approach is to give you a checklist of "points-of-view" that you might consider for your problem. Table 3-5 is such a checklist.

a. For the "Case of the Dinged Stop Sign," brainstorm 15 issues you might consider

under each of the following general viewpoints:
- population perspective;
- political perspective;
- 5W's and H with IS and IS NOT.

b. Repeat for the Problem on which you are working.

3.2 The following activity, from MPS **4** on strategies, gives you a chance to get feedback on how you apply and use a strategy. The objective is for you to obtain a graphical recording of the sequence in which you use the different stages in the MPS 6-stage strategy; the amount of time you spend in each stage and the amount of monitoring you use. Examples are given in Figure 3-7. In example a) the problem solver spent about 4 minutes reading the problem, then 1 minute planning and 12 minutes doing. No monitoring (as shown with inverted triangles) was displayed. The activity is illustrated in Figure 3-8 and is as follows:

a. Pair up with a partner.

b. Review the terminology for the MPS 6-stage strategy so that both agree as to the implicit and explicit activities that are consistent with each of the 6 stages given in Figure 3-4.

c. For a 10 minute period, one plays the **role of a problem solver**. He/she talks aloud (so that there are fewer than two, 10 second silent periods), moves a marker on the strategy board (given in Figure 3-4) to show which stage he/she is now applying and tries to explicitly say the questions and comments related to monitoring. "Let's see, where am I now? Am I finished with this stage? Where now? What did I learn...?" Your partner plays the **role of the listener/recorder**. He/she encourages verbalization, may ask questions so as to understand what the talker is "thinking" (but doesn't interrupt to try to get the problem solver to use the listener's approach), records on the stage-time diagram, of Figure 3-9, the number of minutes spent in each stage (as

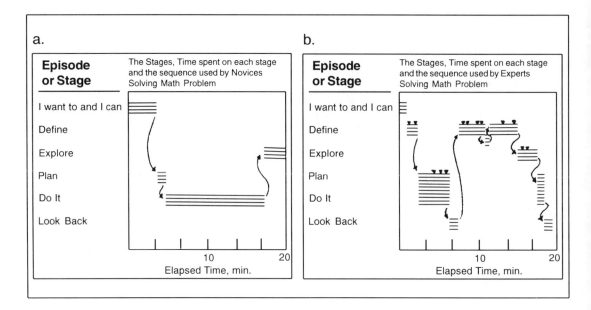

Figure 3-7 Stage-time charts of two problem solvers

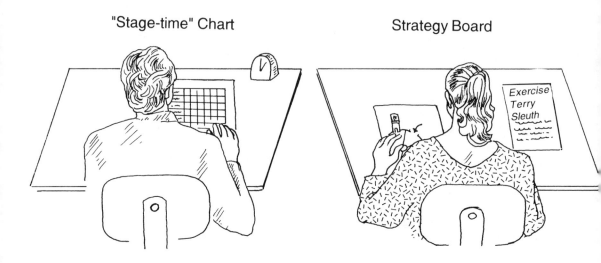

Figure 3-8 Two participants engaged in the process

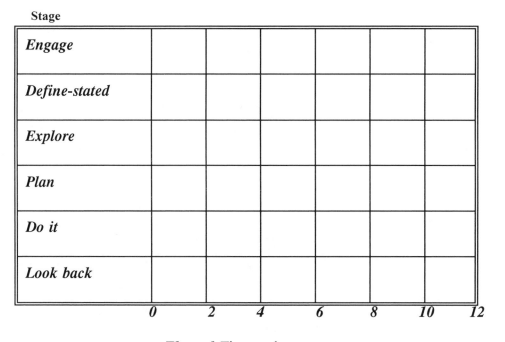

Stage

Engage						
Define-stated						
Explore						
Plan						
Do it						
Look back						

0   2   4   6   8   10   12

Elapsed Time, min.

Figure 3-9 Stage-time chart

shown by the marker), and notes, via a triangle, all explicit monitoring statements.

    d. After the 10 minutes, each should privately reflect on the process used and then take 2 minutes to discuss the process with each other.

    e. Reverse roles and repeat the activity.

Example exercises that can be used by the problem solver are given in Table 3-7.

3.3 Return to the Case "It Just Happens" and apply what you have learned about problem solving to describes your processes. Give yourself feedback by monitoring your problem-solving processes for a week. Use Table 3-6. Reflect on what you discover; add your reflections to your journal.

Feedback:

Figure 3-7a shows the stage-time diagram for an unsuccessful problem solver; Figure 3-7b, for a successful problem solver. During the first minutes of her script, the successful problem solver displays the typical "exercise-solving pattern"; then she tackles the tough portion - a real problem. Note the amount of time spent in explore, the backtracking and the amount of monitoring (as shown by the inverted triangles).

Table 3-7 Terry Sleuth Exercises

Terry Sleuth and the Case of the Missing Jewels
(based on ideas from Jeff M. Elliott, Chris D. Elliott and Steve P. Lake)

"Meow!" The black cat scampered down the alley at the back of Brooks' Jewellers. Terry Sleuth stepped over the glass from the broken window and scrutinized the clever device that short circuited the burglar alarm on the outside wall.

"That certainly would have kept the signal from getting to headquarters," remarked the Sleuth.

Inside the store, Terry talked to owner, Jed Brooks. "That's the third robbery this year! and the most devastating. They took the best jewellery from both the cases and the safe. It's a good job I took out insurance a couple of months ago," Jed noted as he wiped perspiration from his brow.

"Looks like an inside job, or some careless talk," suggested Sergeant Bob Briggs. "Whoever did this really knew the details of the alarm and the safe."

"I can't believe my present employees Judy or Latif could have done it," said Jed. "Although, Judy is heading off to the Caribbean on an expensive cruise next week. And then there's Marj. Business has not been that great. I had to fire Marj two weeks ago. She was very upset."

"I can imagine she would be; she had been with you for 12 years, hadn't she?" asked Terry.

"Yes, and she was very angry and said, 'I'll get even with you Jed Brooks.'"

Briggs said.. "I'll get the detectives checking out Marj's alibi right away."

"Just a minute," suggested Terry. What does Terry see?

Terry Sleuth and the Case of the Town Bypass

As the Sleuth wandered into the office, Detective Sergeant Bob Briggs remarked, "Too bad about Dr. Harrison's wife, eh. Died last week. Heart attack the coroner said." "Poor little rich girl," continued Bob, oblivious as to whether Terry was listening or not, "She must have been under so much strain looking after her estate of $6 million."

"Yes," noted the Sleuth, "Harrison certainly wasn't making that amount of money. I understand that his pharmacy business was not doing that well since the new city bypass was built. Apparently he and city mayor Alan Brignall had strained relationships over that issue."

"I'm not sure we needed the bypass anyway. Of course, Brignall isn't popular with many. Gossip has it that Brignall was having an affair with contractor Harvey Cool's wife and then with councillor Becky Travis. Talking of gossip, I saw Dr. Harrison and Dr. Ahmed, the coroner, in some pretty heady conversation in Elora last weekend," rambled Briggs.

"Perhaps we should look into that more fully," suggested Terry Sleuth.

"Look into what?" asked Bob Briggs.

Terry said... What did Terry say?

4 What is small group, problem-based learning?

Professor Case asks groups of five students:

> "Here's a toaster that isn't working, fix it! or better still, improve it."

On the other hand, Professor Single asks this question of individuals in his course.

Both use problem-based learning. However, Professor Case asks students to work cooperatively and together; Professor Single expects students to study on their own.

In this Chapter we explore some of the advantages and disadvantages of working as individuals as opposed to working in groups.

4.1 What is Small Group, PBL?

A small group is between 3 and 9 students working cooperatively together. Although my preference is about 5 to 6 students, opinions vary. Resource limitations encourage slightly larger-sized groups. Membership in the group may be assigned, or you might have the option to select your group. For the greatest personal growth, it is best if you are assigned to the group.

The more variety in the group (variety of background, experiences, preferred style of processing information) the richer and better the result. However, that very variety will also breed conflict. Conflict that will tear the group apart if

you do not learn how to handle the group dynamics effectively.

All groups must have a chairperson. Research has shown that a group with the weakest person acting as chairperson will outperform groups trying to function without a chairperson. Johnson, Johnson and Smith (1991) suggest that, in addition, group members be assigned such roles as recorder, checker, encourager and elaborator (p. 3-4). My preference is that one person be identified as chairperson and that the group decides whether the group members will have identified roles.

So far, the focus has been on a small group: 3 to 9 people assigned to work together. For each meeting, one person will be chairperson. What about small group PBL? Little more needs to be said other than the small group is brought together to work cooperatively to learn, using a problem to drive the learning.

4.2 Advantages and Disadvantages of Group Work

The advantages and disadvantages are as follows.

4.2-1 Advantages of Using Small Groups

Research has shown that the following conditions foster learning (Chickering and Gamson, 1987; Gibbs, undated and Novak, 1989):
1. Get learners **actively** involved; don't have them listen passively to one speaker.

2. Have learners work cooperatively; make success depend on teamwork and helping each other.

3. Respect diverse talents and ways of learning. Individuals have preferred styles and ways of learning. Not everyone learns things following the same process. For example, some prefer to learn the theory first; then work problems. Others prefer the reverse. Some prefer explanations using pictures, diagrams and charts; some prefer tables, equations, symbols and matrices; some prefer to think in terms of words. Foster learning by allowing and accounting for the individual preferences.

4. Emphasize time on task. Enough time must be available to complete the task; but learners must use the time productively and effectively. Learners should know where they are going, how they will know when they get there and where they are now. There should be clear goals/expectations with measurable criteria to tell when the goal is reached. Both goals and criteria must be achievable with the resources available. Furthermore, students must be motivated to use their time productively.

5. Provide prompt feedback on performance.

6. Empower the learners to have a role in the assessment. Gibbs (undated) says, "Whoever owns the assessment, owns the learning." Novak (1989) identifies assessment as being one of the key ingredients to facilitating learning.

7. Work in an environment that **expects** success.

8. Have frequent and rich tutor-student interaction.

9. Problem solving, group skills and other *processing skills* are not developed by observing others nor by providing "an unstructured opportunity" to do the skill on one's own. Rather, to develop awareness, skill and confidence we need to break the skill into parts, provide an opportunity to try the skill and provide feedback about that effort. Then, target skills should be described, and we should be given feedback and practice until we master the skill.

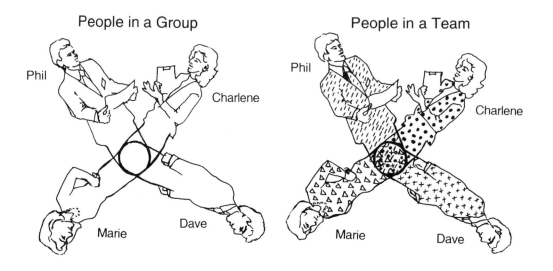

People in a Group

Phil

Charlene

Marie

Dave

People in a Team

Phil

Charlene

Marie

Dave

Figure 4-1 Members of a group versus members of a team

So why work in groups? In brief, you learn better (Johnson, Johnson and Smith, 1991). Groups provide a super opportunity to have active, cooperative learning with prompt informal feedback. Indeed, with care they can provide, through group activities, most of the above components that facilitate learning.

In addition, working in groups will develop your personal skill in working in teams and groups, in coping with conflict, in being a chairperson, in improving your social skills, in developing your interdependence and accountability and in developing your sense of sense worth.

Group work, in school, prepares you well for life-after-graduation.

4.2-2 Disadvantages to Working in Groups

So, if group work is so great, why don't we do it for all courses?

Because it's hard work. Because it often appears to be "unfair": two people do all the work but the slackers get all the credit. Third, to gain advantage of the group learning listed above, we really are talking **team** work and not just *group* work.

Developing effective teams is hard work, demands skill and dedication from all team members and takes time. Perhaps, we lack the interpersonal and group skills to make it work. Perhaps, members are afraid to risk letting their skills and talents be known.

Figure 4-1 shows four people in a group. However, they will not risk possible conflict. Each puts on a smiley face and never risks venturing beyond the central area of common agreement. The net result is, in terms of productivity, $2 + 2 = 3$. The individual performance would have been better than the team performance. Members of a team, on the other hand, risk bringing their special skills, experiences, knowledge, background, preferred style and hangups to the group. They have found ways to cope positively with the conflict the differences bring. The team welcomes and draws on the

diversity. The net result is $2 + 2 = 7$. The output from the team far surpasses what could have been achieved if the task had been done individually.

4.3 Making the Most of the Small Group PBL Format

From a learning viewpoint, all research points to the advantage of the small group, PBL format. We learn more, we learn better. We learn interpersonal, team and team building skills that are needed for a lifetime. However, to make the most of this approach, we need to be skilled at interpersonal relations, communication, groups, team and team building and coping positively with conflict.

4.4 Summary

We learn more effectively and efficiently if we work actively and cooperatively to learn knowledge. Yet, working in groups is hard work. For groups to be effective we need to be skilled in interpersonal relations and in group process.

4.5 References

Chickering, A.W., and Z.F. Gamson (1987) "Seven Principles for good practice in undergraduate education," AAHE Bulletin, March, 3-7.

Gibbs, Graham (undated) "A-Z of Student Focused Teaching Strategies," Educational Methods Unit, Oxford Polytechnic, Headington, UK.

Johnson, D.W., R.T. Johnson and K.A. Smith (1991) "Active Learning: cooperation in the college classroom," Interaction Book, Edina, MN.

Novak, J. (1989) "Helping students learn how to learn: a view from a teacher-researcher," Third Congress of Research and Teaching in Science and Mathematics, Santiago de Compostela, Spain, Sept. reviewed in PS News **69**.

4.6 Exercises

4.1 List 25 things that you don't like about group work. Then brainstorm ways to overcome each. You might use Kurt Lewin's Force-field diagram approach to display your results. (Lewin's force-field approach is illustrated in University Associates Annual '73, p 111 or Structured Experiences, II, p 79. published by University Associates, San Diego, CA.)

4.2 With your group, brainstorm the things that might make working together frustrating. Agree on policies to handle each.

5 *Group skills*

Arnie's group

"I hate this group! No one pulls their weight. I have to do it all," complained Arnie bitterly to the tutor.

"You will be with this group for the next 6 weeks. Perhaps you should take some time away from the PBL and focus on your interpersonal and group skills," suggested the tutor.

"What do you mean?" asked a puzzled Arnie.

We walk into a room and are placed in a group. Something magical is supposed to happen. We are supposed to work together effectively, drawing on each other's strengths, supporting each other's weaknesses, getting the task done and ending the activity not wanting to part.

All the groups I worked with were the pits! We started out OK. Then, Jeff started to skip meetings. Michelle was unreliable and put the emphasis on other things. Peter came, but just wasn't prepared. and Harry! He complained and took cheap shots at all of us. I could hardly wait to get out of that group.

In small group PBL you will be working in groups.

For this situation, what do you know already about group work?

Perhaps you already are skilled in working in groups. You know how to motivate group members, to keep the morale high no matter what happens. You know how to handle conflict effectively. Perhaps you have already had extensive experience. If you know all of the issues and details for this situation already, skip to the next Chapter.

For this situation, what are the issues?

Some of the issues, for effective group work, are illustrated in Figure 5-1. In particular, these are:

1. Know yourself, your strengths, your weaknesses and your preferences and to become comfortable with yourself;

2. Value the diversity in others;

3. Know and apply the fundamental underpinnings of interpersonal relations;

4. Be a good, empathetic communicator;

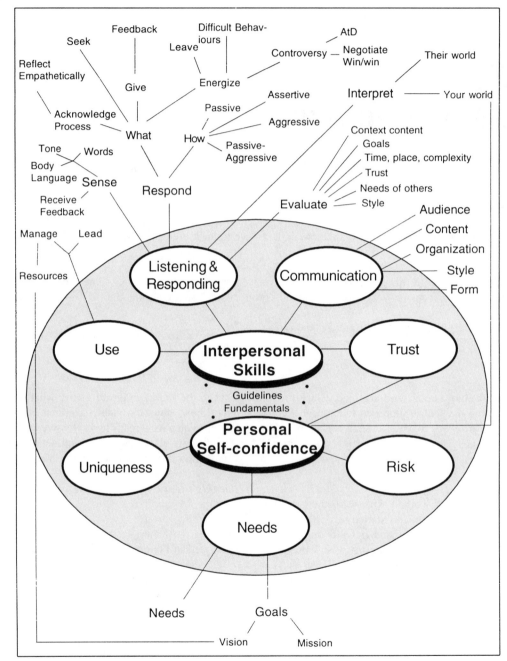

Figure 5-1 Issues in group skills

5. Know the attributes of groups, to know how you function in a group;

6. Know the role of the chairperson and be skilled in playing that role for the group;

7. Know how to cope creatively with conflict;

8. Know hope to cope effectively with difficult behaviours; and

9. Know how to convert a group into a team.

Each of these issues is considered in turn. You may wish to go directly to the section that answers your needs.

5.1. Be Comfortable with Yourself and Value Diversity in Others

"Be proud of who you are and how you do things." That's easy to say; perhaps, hard to do. Usually, we move from self-awareness to self-acceptance. The Myers-Briggs Type indicator or Jungian typology instrument is a good inventory to help you see how you make decisions (P-J dimension), what facts you feature in thinking about issues (S-N and T-F dimensions) and how you prefer to validate ideas (I-E dimension) (MBTI, Hogan and Champagne, 1974, Keirsey and Bates, 1984). Your self-talk is also revealing. If you tend to praise yourself - as opposed to criticize - you probably manage stress well and have a positive self-image. In brief, improve your self-esteem and be comfortable with yourself by:
- becoming aware of your style;
- cultivating the qualities you like in yourself;
- learning to enjoy being alone;
- developing your capacity for pleasure;
- being positive, smiling and avoiding cynicism;
- believing in yourself;
- being willing to confront people when you disagree with them about something that matters to you;
- remembering that you are what you create.

If you need to know more about this topic, Woods and Ormerod (1993) give practical suggestions and list other resources.

As we learn more about ourselves and our preferred way of doing things, we learn to value the diversity in others. If we tend to make decisions hastily, we need input from those who prefer to gain extensive data before deciding. Those with science and mathematical backgrounds treasure the insight from someone with language, philosophy and nursing backgrounds. In other words, as we take pride in our own approaches, we value more the richness that others bring to group discussion.

5.2 Live the Fundamental Underpinnings of Interpersonal Relationships

Honour the seven fundamental personal rights, follow the guidelines to interpersonal *Shangri La*, build trust and communicate empathetically - these are the fundamental underpinnings.

5.2-1 Rules of Conduct: the Seven Fundamental Personal Rights

We all have right to choose, to have opinions, to be respected, to have needs, to have and express feelings, to make mistakes (and be forgiven) and to accept these rights in others. These seven fundamental personal rights are the foundation of all of our interpersonal behaviour. These are crucial to understanding how to listen and respond, how to manage stress, how to cope effectively with anger and how to deal with those difficult behaviours we encounter in life. These rights are the basis of negotiation and assertiveness. They are crucial for "self-esteem".

5.2-2 Guidelines for Conduct: Achieving Interpersonal *Shangri La*

Here are nine guidelines for conduct:

1. We all are unique, can function from the point of their individual past experience, and are

valued because of our uniqueness. Show respect for the person as an individual.

2. The golden rule is still golden: treat others the way you would like to be treated.

3. Look for the good in others; expect the best.

4. If you don't have anything nice to say, don't say anything at all.

5. Be loyal first to yourself and then to others.

6. Maintain a sense of humour; keep things in perspective.

7. Cooperation must be earned, not demanded.

8. People don't care how much you know.. just how much you care about them.

9. Show empathy; indicate that you have listened and understood others. Focus the response on being flexible so that you show willingness to listen and try to understand another's views.

5.2-3 Guidelines for Growth Through Feedback: Other Guidelines Toward Interpersonal *Shangri La*

To improve, we need feedback. We need others to share with us how we can improve. Indeed, it is usually not hard to find people willing to give us advice. Our human tendency is one of **judging** others **and** telling them! Our goal is to corral that tendency to judge others; to learn how to respond to positive feedback; and to learn how to give constructive feedback to others for growth.

a. Giving Positive Feedback for Growth

10. Identify **5** strengths for every **2** things you feel they might wish to change. Feedback is 5 "warm fuzzies" and 2 to work on. This is exemplified, for example, on the bottom of Feedback form Table 3-6.

11. Provide positive feedback often, honestly and as soon as possible after the noteworthy event.

b. Responding to Positive Feedback

12. Say "Thank you".

c. Giving "Negative" Feedback for Growth

Consider Why? What? How? and When?

Why?

13. For feedback, focus on the **value** it will be to the **recipient** rather than on the *power* or *release* it provides to the person giving the feedback.

What?

14. For feedback, give the amount of information the person can productively use (rather than the amount you want to unload on them all at once).

15. Focus feedback on the person's *behaviour* and not on his/her personality. Be problem oriented not personality oriented. Separate the people and personalities from the behaviours. Separate the "person" from the "offence." Replace "you are a biased person" with "when you select Jim to do the job instead of me, I see that as an biased act."

16. Focus on *descriptions* of behaviours and not on advice, or judgements about the behaviour. (Unless, because of your position, you must provide a judgement. When asked for advice, it usually is better to help explore options rather than give **your** answer to the problem.)

17. Focus on your observations rather than your inferences, interpretations, conclusions or judgements. Say, "Here is what I observe.." Focus on **what** is said and not **why** it is said.

18. Describe behaviours in terms that place them on a continuum between "low" and "high" or

"large" and "small" rather than in terms of "either/or". For example, participation may be "low" or "high" rather than "yes" or "no".

19. Show ownership of the ideas, and opinions: use words that show ownership "I" or "you" rather than "some people" or "we".

20. Cite a specific situation rather than an abstract behaviour.

21. Cite "here and now" and not on "there and then". No recriminations for past events.

How?

22. Focus on being "equality" oriented rather than "superiority" oriented.

23. No shouting, table pounding, foul language, or personal attacks.

When?

24. There is a time and place for everything. Consider whether now is the time and the place. For feedback, the recipient must be ready for it.

General Responses

25. Focus the response to be "at the same intimacy and intensity" (when pertinent). For example, if they shout at you, don't shout back; but if they are fairly excited about an issue, don't be too laid back. They might interpret this as being indifferent or if they start describing innermost feelings; share some feelings too.

26. Give the feedback assertively (not passively or aggressively). You might use the pattern:
    "When you (describe the concrete act), I feel.. (disclose your feelings).. because... (describe a tangible effect).

d. Responding to Negative Feedback

Negative feedback, by its very name, hurts! Even if we call it "areas to work on." So how do we handle it? First, only through feedback can we modify **our** behaviour.

27. Assume the intent is to help you improve. Say "Thanks for your feedback". Perhaps they suggest how you might change your behaviour. One might respond:
    "Thanks for your feedback. I'm sorry that my actions were interpreted that way. It was not my intent. How might I modify what I do?"
    Resist the temptation to elaborate, justify and rationalize.

28. Take it with a grain of salt. You can't please everyone. You need to be yourself. The "Can't Please Everyone Rule" is "10% are going to hate what you do, no matter how hard you try. 10% will think you can walk on water! Look at feedback from the middle 80%."

In summary, 28 suggestions for conduct will lead to interpersonal *Shangri La*. If you need to learn more about these ideas, I recommend Bolton (1979); Cawood (1988); Fritchie (undated). In addition, the McMaster Problem Solving program that complements this book gives workshops in the following units: MPS **52**, "Interpersonal skills;" MPS **44**, "Assertiveness;" and MPS **43**, "Giving and receiving feedback."

5.2-4 Trust is the Glue That Builds Relationships

Trust is the reduction of one's fear of betrayal, disloyalty and rejection; trust promotes the hope of acceptance, support, confirmation and cooperation (Johnson, 1986). Covey (1989) offers a very useful analogy or model of "trust". He sees "trust" between two people as being the "emotional bank account" that one builds up within the other person. When the bank account balance is high, trust is high. When the account is overdrawn, the trust is low. We build up the "trust" account through deposits in the form of actions that:

1. Show that we really seek to understand the other person. We empathize with them. We see the world through their frame of reference. (We accept them **as they are**, warts and all; we don't have to agree with it; but we understand and accept it.)

2. Attend to the little kindnesses and courtesies of life.

3. Keep our commitments to ourselves and to others.

4. Clarify expectations we have of ourselves and of others.

5. Show personal honesty and integrity, loyalty to others, especially when they are not present.

6. Promptly show that we know when we are wrong through sincere apologies.

7. Follow the seven fundamental personal rights and the guidelines to interpersonal *Shangri La.*

We risk when we "deposit". We risk that the other might exploit us, ridicule or reject our actions. Trust develops when the "deposits" are graciously accepted. Trust develops further when the other person reciprocates. In other words, if you self-disclose personal opinions, the other will also self-disclose when such is pertinent.

If there is one key to building trust and to good interpersonal skills, it is how we **listen and respond**. We need to communicate empathetically.

5.2-5 Communicate Empathetically

A basic skill for effective interpersonal skill is the ability to listen and to respond. In particular, to listen and respond in such a way that you express yourself and you show that you understand the needs, feelings and opinions of others. Steil et al.

(1985) propose a four-stage model of the listening process (**SIER**).

Sensing: In sensing, we often use the four senses of seeing, hearing, touching and smelling. Sometimes we also taste; taste a gourmet meal. Occasionally, some might invoke a sixth sense. Surprisingly, messages are communicated about 50% by body langauge, about 40% by the tone and only 10% by the actual words themselves. Sensing the "true" message from another is not a trivial task. We need to "attend" (pay full attention to that person) and track and follow (react so that the talker is aware that we are listening).

Interpret: We match our internal meaning of words with the sounds and images we sense. We interpret the sensed message **in the context of our internal mental and emotional view of the world.** Contrast this with the other person who expresses the message in the context of his/her view of the world. To interpret the message we must empathize; see the message from their view of the world. Often we need to try to understand that view by "reflecting" their message back to them to check that we comprehend their true intent.

Evaluate: We assess the validity and relevance within the context. Before we decide **what** and **how** to respond, we must evaluate what we have interpreted. The general criteria used in the evaluation are based on what we want to Achieve, Preserve and Avoid. In general we want to

Achieve answers to our problems and achieve our personal goals.

Preserve self-respect, the rights of others and good interpersonal relations, and

Avoid the breakup of relationships, distrust and heartache.

To be more specific, the criteria used to evaluate the situation and select a response include the following:

1. The content and context: what has gone on in the past and what seems to be needed as the next phase.

2. Your goal.

3. The time, place and the complexity of the issues.

4. The amount of trust and cooperation among the people.

5. Your style (of listening and responding, your preference in handling disagreements, your preference in processing information and prioritizing issues). Two inventories help us to see our preferred way of using information. (Johnson's preferred style of responding to conflict (Johnson, 1986) and Jungian Typology (Hogan and Champagne, 1974 or Keirsey and Bates, 1984)). Figure 5-2 gives the results of Johnson's preferred response to conflict. The five responses he suggests are 1) Accommodate, 2) Compromise, 3) Collaborate/problem solve / negotiate, 4) Withdraw and 5) Force. Shown in bold numerals are the responses from 43 engineers and managers; in bold italics, the responses from 31 second year engineering students; in arabic numerals, the responses from 65 leaders of the Girl Guides of Canada. Your style affects primarily the *content* of your responses and the issues you feel are important.

6. You and them. Your mood and needs; their mood and needs.

Respond: We indicate, appropriately, what we have sensed; or how we wish to proceed with the talking-listening process. Our options are responses to:

    acknowledge;
    seek/ask;
    give/supply;
    energize/divert.

Some of these responses are illustrated in Figure 5-2.

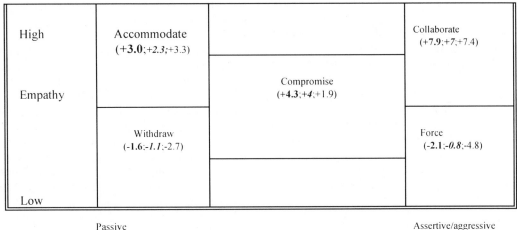

High	Accommodate (**+3.0**;*+2.3*;+3.3)			Collaborate (**+7.9**;*+7*;+7.4)
			Compromise (**+4.3**;*+4*;+1.9)	
Empathy				
	Withdraw (-1.6;*-1.1*;-2.7)			Force (**-2.1**;*-0.8*;-4.8)
Low				

Passive   Assertive/aggressive

Approach to Task

Figure 5-2 Some response options for energize/divert

In summary, good listening and responding skills are crucial for strong interpersonal and group skills. This four-stage model gives a framework for reflecting on the process. This same framework is used to provide a framework for giving feedback about the group process.

5.3 Be A Valued Member of the Group

Here are seven characteristics of valued members of a group.

5.3-1 Attend to Both Morale and Task Components

Any group has two responsibilities: to uplift, sustain and enrich the **morale** of the group members and of the group, and to complete a **task**. Both are required. Indeed, our research shows that, with rare exceptions, one affects the other. If the task is not completed, the morale will be low; if the morale is low, the task is usually not completed. Figure 5-3 shows that groups' self-ratings of the morale and task are closely related.

Valued members understand the task and morale components and do their best to have both of these positive. Table 5-1 notes four dimensions for each:

- acknowledge/observer the process: (how the people are interacting and how the problem solving process to complete the task is being done);

- giver of input: (comments and information to positively improve interpersonal interactions and subject knowledge to complete the task);

- asker or seeker of input: (asks for information to improve interpersonal relations and to complete the task);

- energizer/diverter: (brings a new dimension, tension relief, new insight).

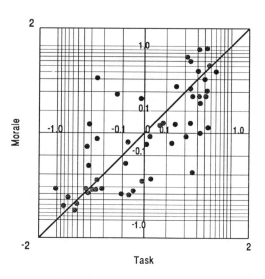

Figure 5-3 Morale and task ratings interact

Descriptions of both positive and negative behaviour are listed. Most groups need all eight dimensions. Any group member can provide the dimension. Indeed, as the meeting proceeds, many different people could provide "task information giver". Often, we would call the person at that time, "the leader".

5.3-2 Don't Fight for Leadership; Leadership Rotates Among Members

Leadership rotates among group members depending on who has the most to offer at a particular time. Whoever has the most pertinent experience will be called on by the group to provide leadership. Sometimes the leadership evolves as the group solves problems. Leadership develops because of technical experience and knowledge, because of special problem solving abilities such as the ability to dream up ideas or see the situation from a completely different perspective, because of monitoring and organizational skills or because of people skills.

The chairperson, on the other hand, has prime responsibility for the roles of morale and task process observer and morale and task seeker.

5.3-3 Help the Chairperson to be Effective

Research has shown that groups that select their chairperson at random will outperform those groups who have no chairperson (Dimock, 1970).

Select a chairperson. (Most student groups in PBL assume that the tutor is the chairperson. This robs the students of the chance to develop their skill and develop their self-confidence. Having the tutor as chairperson undermines the role of the tutor and weakens the empowerment of the group.) Choose a student chairperson.

The chairperson facilitates growth. During the meeting the chairperson monitors, reminds the group of time schedules and agreed-upon "norms" of behaviour and maintains decorum. The chairperson monitors to identify when things are slightly awry. He/she must decide whether to be neutral and "let the group get on with the task" or to intercede positively to bring it back onto track.

The chairperson must prepare an agenda. My "Agenda rule" is "No detailed agenda; no attendance." Meetings are the greatest waste of time that was ever invented. The saying "If you want to kill an idea, give it to a committee!" is true. **Your** meetings will be different. Group members need to support the chairperson's efforts to do the following (and, if he/she doesn't, to gently nudge her/him into action):

Table 5-1 Feedback about roles in a group

			Group Members							
Task										
Observer -	Task Process	Orients group, monitors, summarizes, seeks direction, identifies phases +								
		Ignores phases, asks whatever wants, blocks, unaware of contributions -								
Giver -	Information Opinion	Assertively gives information, makes suggestions +								
		Withholds information, silent, aggressive or passive								
Seeker -	Information Opinion	Asks questions/for opinion; checks comprehension +								
		Refuses to ask for information, silent -								
Energizer -	Risk Taker	Enthusiastic, introduces spark, novel ideas +								
		Follower, agrees, silent, unsure -								
Morale										
Observer -	Interpersonal Process	Sensitive to interpersonal dynamics, comments on +								
		Ignores conflicts and tension, hopes it disappears								
Giver -	Praise, Support	Warm, responsive, gives help, rewards +								
		Put downs, aggressive, self-centered, defensive -								
Seeker -	Interpersonal Problem Solver	Mediates, harmonizes, helps resolve conflicts +								
		Causes problems, seeks personal goals -								
Energizer -	Tension Relief	Jokes, laughs, shows satisfaction +								
		Withdraws, causes tension -								

from D.R. Woods. "How to Gain the Most from PBL." (1994)

- create agendas that are meaningful for your group;

- address procedural issues such as:

1. how we will make decisions (vote? consensus?);

2. the names for the problem solving stages (MPS 6-stage described in Chapter 3?);

3. the role of chairperson (see that the group makes a decision? or concur with the group's decision? vote or not vote? method of reaching consensus?);

4. the resources required for each meeting and who supplies (coffee? flipchart? overhead transparencies and pens?);

5. the method of recording decisions and information and by whom (minutes? with an **Action** column where the initials of the person responsible for completing the action are given? when distribute?);

6. the meeting format: (prioritize issues and identify time allowed?);

7. the process for dealing with conflict; policies; method of addressing one another; and

8. the process for asking a member to leave the group and the consequences. Part of this may be beyond the group's control; however, identify who has the control and meet with them to evolve policies.

5.3-4: Help the Group Evolve Through the Maturing Process

Valued members facilitate group growth. Groups don't start off terrifically. At the start group members are asking, "Why am I in this group?", "Am I accepted as being a welcome member in this group?". As the group matures, the concerns shift to questions like,"who controls this group? how close to I want to get emotionally to the group members?". The usual stages of group evolution are illustrated in Table 5-2: forming, storming,

Table 5-2 Issues as a group evolves

Stages in evolution

Focus in each stage	Form Orient	Storm Conflict Control	Norm Emerge Affection	Perform Reinforce Team	Part Separate
Task	All agree; tend to make vague, ambiguous comments.	Nitpick, polarize, challenge.	Use ambiguity as an outlet for dissent.	Strong agreement as to task; make decisions by consensus.	
Morale	Am I in this group?	Who controls?	Am I comfortable in this group? How close do I want to get?	Conflict improves our answers; conflict helps build trust.	What happens now?

norming, performing and parting. Some issues that pertain to morale and task are featured in the table. Schutz's FIRO-B instrument may give you insight as to the roles you might play in nurturing the evolution. (Details about FIRO-B are given by Whetten and Cameron, 1984, and Ryan, 1970.)

The main idea here is that groups don't start off great. They evolve. Being aware of that evolutionary process fosters understanding and progress for group members.

5.3-5 Assume the Roles the Group Needs

Valued members are aware of their contributions. Each of us has preferred roles we are most comfortable assuming. However, we should be skilled and willing to assume other roles as we become aware of the group needs.

5.3-6 Reflect on Each Meeting

Take time, at the end of each meeting, to discuss how well the morale and task components of the group were handled. Then ask each member, in turn, to comment on the role he/she felt they played. This should be for clarification; not heated discussion. List your group's five strengths and the two areas to work on. Use this reflection time and goal setting activity to help the group see growth from meeting to meeting.

5.3-7 Let Others Know of Complications

If you cannot attend; if you have not done your homework; if you have to leave early; if you might be late - let your chairperson know.

5.3-8 Clarify the Role of the Tutor

In some groups, we assume that the tutor is "automatically" the chairperson. If the tutor sits at the "head" of the table; if no one speaks until the tutor has spoken- these are some of the signals that infer that the tutor is the chairperson. Is this the role the tutor should have for the growth of your group?

When conflict occurs, when the morale of the group drags, when we don't seem to be on task, do you expect the tutor to sort things out for you?

Clarify the role of the tutor in your PBL group at this particular time in your growth in PBL.

Dimock (1970), Sampson and Marthas (1990), Johnson and Johnson (1982) and MPS **28** provide more details on group process.

5.4 Be an Effective Chairperson

Every group must have a chairperson. The chairperson is **not** the leader; the chairperson is the facilitator. The chairperson anticipates the needs of the group meeting; prepares an agenda and then facilitates the group process. At times, the chairperson assumes the role of leader when her/his experience related to the task is required.

5.4-1 Anticipate the Needs of the Group

Groups need to know when and where they are going to meet. Members should know who is going to attend and why they are a member of the group. These details and arrangements should be made ahead of time by the chairperson. They should know, in some detail, the purpose of the meeting, the background issues that they should consider, what each should do to prepare for the meeting and what they should bring to the meeting.
If the issue is particularly contentious, the chairperson should himself/herself (or delegate others to) work through the problem as best he/she can and share those ideas with the members ahead of time.

5.4-2 Prepare the Agenda

The agenda should be sent to all group members well ahead of the meeting. It must include:
Where: location (with map if necessary),

When: time and day and duration of meeting,
Purpose:
List of participants:
Premeeting preparation:
Please bring:
Agenda: sequencing of topics with time allotted for each item.
Table 5-3 gives a sample agenda.

5.4-3 Facilitate the Meeting

Be there well ahead of time. Check that the facilities are as you requested. Bring along extra copies of the agenda. Out of courtesy of those who are on time, start the meeting on time. End the meeting on time. Adapt the mental attitude that you are there to help the group succeed. (You are not there to *get your ideas accepted*.) Two additional suggestions are:

a. Apply Bernice Sandler's rule "After 20 min of discussion on one topic, the group is usually ready to a) make a decision or b) identify the information it is lacking to make a good decision." After 20 min, you begin to hear the same people restating their original arguments (but a bit more vehemently).

Table 5-3 A sample agenda (used with permission)

AGENDA - SDL-1 PLANNING SESSION

PURPOSE: Given the overall problem, plan a method for acquiring the needed knowledge using self-directed learning concepts.

TYPE OF MEETING: Planning.
WHEN: Monday, Oct 26, 1992 at 13:30
WHERE: JHE 342.
WHO:
  Kyle Bouchard
  MaryLynne DeGuili
  Michelle Gretzinger - Chairperson
  Craig Norman
  Steve Skippen

PREMEETING PREPARATION:
Read: - "More Skills for PS" Chapter 6.
         - Overall problem and resources for Unit 3 in Phase IV Workbook. (The first white pages past the greens.)
         - Overall course objectives 4, 5, 6, 7, and 10 (from the first day handout).

OBJECTIVES:
1. Create learning contract: diagnose needs, translate into objectives, identify resources and suggest evidence to show accomplishment.

2. Assign topics to group members for learning individually and teaching to the group on Thursday.

AGENDA:

1. Introduction- allocate roles, review purpose and objectives, review agenda, establish ground rules (input from the group). 5 min.
2. Read over problem. 3 min.
3. Create learning contract. 30 min.
4. Divide learning and teaching responsibilities. 5 min.
5. Chairperson assessment. 7 min.

---

b. Don't let the group try to rework a subcommittee's report. If a subcommittee has reported to the group about an in-depth study, the group should accept, reject or send back for reevaluation because a key issue was not considered.

5.4-4 Seek Feedback

Take time, at the end of each meeting, for the group to assess how well they did as a group (as outlined in Section 5-3.7) and for all to give the chairperson feedback on the extent to which he/she was:

positive in helping the struggling group to soar (1 for slightly to 10 for fantastically);

negative by preventing, interfering and impeding group process (1 for slightly to 10 for outrageously);

positive neutral and allowed us to get on effectively with the job (1 for slightly to 10 for extensively);

negative neutral because he/she allowed us to wallow in ineffective bickering when strong facilitation skills were needed (1 for slightly to 10 for extensively).

Our experience is that most chairpersons tend to be "neutral" when indeed they are seen as being **negative neutral**.

5.5 Cope Creatively with Conflict

When groups mature, when trust develops, when people risk offering their true talents, differences in ideas, approaches, styles and opinions will occur. Good groups will say **Hurrah!** because from conflict will come better decisions. Poor groups will try to ignore the conflict and hope it goes away.

First, an attitude shift is needed; not all conflicts are bad. Through differences we grow; we build trust because conflicts offer us an opportunity to try

understand where the other person is coming from. We can treasure the diversity of others and grow from that.

Second, there is not just one way to deal with conflict. How to deal with conflict depends. Although each of us has a preferred mode of dealing with conflict (as exemplified by the data in Figure 5-2) there are times when:

- we should withdraw; (when a drunk accosts us and flings insults at us);
- we should force (when fire hits our house and all should vacate immediately; don't negotiate, get out!);
- and so on.

Thus, we should become skilled at using all five types of responses to conflict shown in Figure 5-2. We should select the appropriate response by applying the six criteria outlined in Section 5.2-5. (Content and context, your goal, time, place and complexity, trust, your style, and you and them).

Buehlman et al. (1992) and Gottman (1993) found that responses to conflict that damaged relationships the most were:

- criticism,
- contempt,
- defensiveness, and
- stonewalling or withdrawal.

In relationships, the use of the above "negative" responses must to be counterbalanced by at least five positives for every one "negative" if good relationships are to be regained.

If you need to learn more about coping with conflict, read the MPS Unit **45** in the McMaster Problem Solving program that complements this book.

5.6 Modify your Response to Difficult Behaviours

Many books have been written about "Coping with difficult people". The people aren't difficult; their behaviours are. First, we follow *Shangri La* principle #15 and focus on the behaviour and not the person.

Why are people's behaviour difficult? People have developed "difficult behaviours" because by using them they get their goals. For example, if Tom doesn't get his way, he shouts. He insults us. He makes a scene. To prevent the scene, we let him have his way. "Don't cross Tom; he explodes," you are warned. Difficult behaviours are finely polished. They are skilled performances. You can't change them. But, you can change how you respond to their difficult behaviour. When they see that their difficult behaviour doesn't work for you, then they probably - probably - will stop trying it. Secondly, then, don't try to change them. Rather, change your response to their difficult behaviour.

What is a difficult behaviour? Ruhl (1988) suggests that, although over 84 difficult behaviours have been identified, these can be classified into four basic groups (Warriors, Wimps, Wafflers and Whiners) with 10 subgroups. Other authors (Bramson, 1981; Rhode, 1989; Solomon, 1990; Cava, 1990; Brinkman and Kirschner, undated) use other terms and classifications. We see these are extreme extensions of one's style in coping with conflict. Figure 5-4 extends the five options, shown in Figure 5-2, to create eight general types. Having a name or characteristic and basis for the behaviour helps us to select a strategy for responding to that behaviour.

In responding to the behaviour,

1. Recall the model for anger presented in Chapter 1. Inappropriate thoughts and responses only trigger a cycle of escalation. (Figure 1-2 illustrates this cycle.) Break the cycle. Do not respond negatively or tit for tat. Manage anger. Control yourself first; then focus on the value of your relationship.

2. Check whether it is really a difficult behaviour. Check whether you are the exhibiting it or they. Check whether they are aware of what they are doing. Respond reflectively and assertively.

3. If it is a difficult behaviour in them, then, modify your responses. Although good

High	"Yes" people	Grenades			"Know it alls"
		Accommodate		Collaborate	
			Compromise		
empathy	Pessimist, silent-ones	Withdraw		Force	Sniper
Low	Chronic complainer	Grenades			Tanks

Figure 5-4: Difficult behaviours are extensions of energize/divert options for response

response patterns are similar, different behaviours call for slight variations. For detailed suggestions on how to cope with specific types of difficult behaviour, I recommend Brinkman and Kirschner's (undated) videotape.

5.7 Build a Team

Table 5-4 summarizes the differences between a group and a team. Figure 5-5 summarizes the growth that converts a group into a team. Both the task and morale components evolve. The task component changes so that agreement is reached on the goals and procedures and monitoring improves. Similarly, the morale components are modified. Table 5-5 provides a feedback form to use for groups.

As teams evolve and are given more responsibility and rights, team and member accountability increase. Freedom and accountability go hand in hand.

For more on teams and team building see Phillips and Elledge, 1989; Francis and Young, 1979 and Scholtes, 1992. (The first two resources focus on the group and people processes; the latter integrates elements of Deming's approach and Total Quality Management.)

5.8 Summary and How to Monitor Progress

Effective groups start with individuals who are self-aware, self-confident and who value the diversity of others. Members live the fundamental principles of interpersonal relationships: honour and claim for themselves the seven fundamental personal rights, they are skilled in the applying the guidelines for interpersonal *Shangri La*, they know the value of and how to give and receive feedback, and they behave so as to build trust.

The SIER model for listening and responding was given. This is the basis for effective communication, for coping with conflict and for dealing with difficult behaviours. The criteria for selecting responses are given.

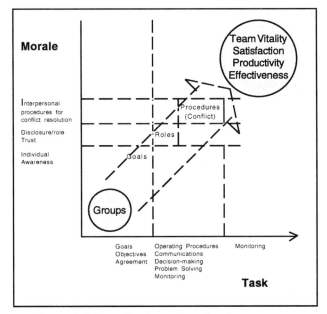

Figure 5-5 Growth of morale and task components

Table 5-4 Comparison of a group with a team

Group	Team
Each represents a different constituency; has his /her own hidden agenda and each may try to get their interest group to benefit at the expense of others.	Each accepts the team goals and willingly foregoes personal and constituent goals for the benefit of the team.
Each unsure of role, other than to represent constituency.	Each has a role to play; each knows the role and the contribution to the team.
Decisions are made by vote. Acceptance of the best for the most dominant interest group	Decisions made by consensus. Acceptance of the best for the team.
If interpersonal conflicts occur, ignore them because "I won't be on this committee forever." The group has not method, other than embarrassment, for resolving conflicts.	Most conflicts must be addressed and resolved. The group has an accepted method of resolving conflicts. The ability to resolve conflicts is a key skill.
If I miss a meeting, so what? who cares?	Must not miss a meeting because you are needed for the success of the team.
All tend to put on a happy face and accept the median or common skills. 2 + 2 = 3.	Team does better than a collection of individual efforts because all contribute all their skills. They accept each other "warts and all". 2+2 =7
"**I**" attitude	"**We**" attitude

The seven characteristics of valued group members are noted: morale and task are both important, leadership is shared, all groups need a chairperson, groups evolve, various roles are needed in the group and monitoring group meetings helps groups mature and become effective teams. Guidelines are given for being an effective chairperson, for coping creatively with conflict, for dealing with difficult behaviours and for building teams.

Table 5-5 is a checklist that can be used to monitor team development.

5.9 References

Bolton, R. (1979) "People Skills," Touchstone Book, Simon and Schuster, New York, NY.

Bransom, R.M. (1981) "Coping with Difficult People in business and life," Ballantine Books, New York, NY.

Brinkman, R. and R. Kirschner (undated) "How to Deal with Difficult People," Careertrak videotape, Boulder CO.

Buehlman, K.T., J.M. Gottman and L.F. Katz (1992) "How Couples View Their Past Predicts Their Future: Predicting Divorce from an Oral History Interview," J. of Family Psychology, **5**, 3 & 4, 295-318.

Cava, R. (1990) "Difficult People," Key Porter Books, Toronto, ON.

Cawood, D. (1988) "Assertiveness for Managers: learning the effective skills for managing people,"

Table 5-5 Feedback for growth in team skills

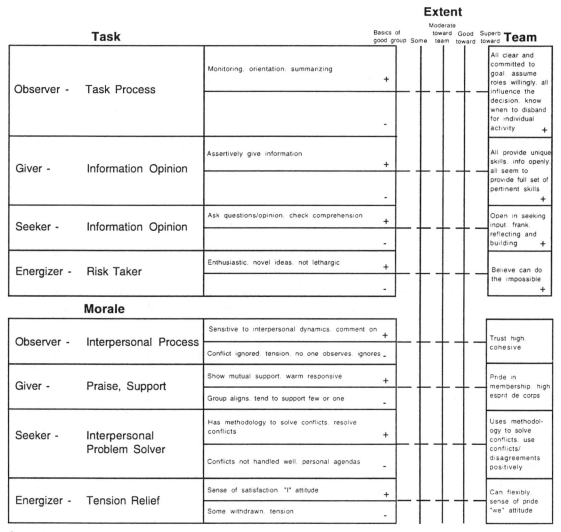

'from D.R.Woods, "How to Gain the Most from PBL," 1994.

2nd ed. Self Counsel Press, Toronto, ON.

Covey, S. R. (1989) "The 7 Habits of Highly Effective People," Fireside Book, Simon and Schuster, New York, NY.

Dimock, H.G. (1970) a series of four booklets: "Factors in Working in Groups," "How to Observe your Group," "How to analyze and evaluate group growth," and "Planning Group development," Sir George Williams Bookstore, Concordia University, Montreal, PQ.

Francis, D., and D. Young (1979) "Improving work groups: a practical manual for team building," University Associates, San Diego, CA.

Fritchie, Rennie (undated) "Working with Assertiveness," BBC. London, UK.

Gottman, J.M. (1993) "The Roles of Conflict Engagement, Escalation and Avoidance in Marital Interaction: a Longitudinal View of Five Types of Couples," J. of Consulting and Clinical Psychology, **61**, 1, 6-15.

Hogan, C., and D. Champagne (1974) "Personal Style Inventory," University Associates Annual, San Diego, CA.

Johnson, D.W. (1986) "Reaching Out," Prentice-Hall, Englewood Cliffs, NJ.

Johnson, D.W., and F.P Johnson (1982) "Joining Together: group theory and group skills," 2nd ed., Prentice-Hall, Englewood Cliffs, NJ.

Keirsey, D. and M. Bates (1984) "Please Understand Me: Character and temperament types," Gnosology Books, Del Mar, CA.

MPS **28**, "Group Skills," Department of Chemical Engineering, McMaster University, Hamilton, ON.

MPS **43**, "Giving and Receiving Feedback," Department of Chemical Engineering, McMaster University, Hamilton, ON.

MPS **44**, "Assertiveness," Department of Chemical Engineering, McMaster University, Hamilton, ON.

MPS **45**, "Coping Creatively with Conflict," Department of Chemical Engineering, McMaster University, Hamilton, ON.

MPS **52**, "Interpersonal Skills," Department of Chemical Engineering, McMaster University, Hamilton, ON.

MPS **53**, "Teams and Team building," Department of Chemical Engineering, McMaster University, Hamilton, ON.

Myers-Briggs Type Indicator (MBTI), Consulting Psychologists Press, 3803 E. Bayshore Rd., Palo Alto, CA, 94303.

Phillips, S.L., and R.L. Elledge (1989) "The Team Building Source Book," University Associates, San Diego, CA.

Ruhl, Anne (1988) workshop on "Influencing difficult people," McMaster University, Hamilton; article "Managing your difficult person," Personnel Matters Newsletter of McMaster University, Dec 1991, p 3. and Jay Gibson (1987).

Rhode, Helga (1989) "Assertiveness Training for Professionals," Career Track videotape, Boulder, CO.

Ryan, L.R. (1970) "Clinical Interpretation of FIRO-B," Consulting Psychologists Press, Palo Alto, CA.

Sampson, E.E. and M. Marthas, (1990) "Group Process for the health professions," 2nd ed., Delmar Publishers Inc., Albany, NY.

Sandler, B. (1988) personal communication.

Scholtes, P.R., (1992) "The Team Handbook: how to use teams to improve quality," Joiner Associates, Inc., Madison, WI.

Schutz, W.C. (1958) "FIRO: a three-dimensional theory of interpersonal behaviour," Holt, Rinehart and Winston, New York, NY. see also Ryan 1970 and Whetten and Cameron, p. 55.

Solomon, M. (1990) "Working with Difficult People," Prentice Hall, Englewood Cliffs, NJ.

Steil, L.K., Summerfield, J. and G. deMare (1985) "Listening: it can change your life," McGraw-Hill paperback, New York, NY.

Whetten, D.A. and K.S. Cameron (1984) "Developing Management Skills," Scott Foresman, Glenview, IL.

Woods, D.R. and S.D. Ormerod (1993) "Networking: how to enrich your life and get things done," Pfeiffer and Co., San Diego, CA.

5.10 Exercises.

5.1 Create a way a group could deal with the following situations:

1. Anne participates in all the meetings but never comes prepared; she does not meet her commitments.

2. Philip is extremely disruptive. He seems to think that he is the only one with ideas. From the very first meeting, he comes on like a freight train!

3. The chairperson Andy is using his position as chair to force decisions only he wants.

5.2 Repeat question 5-1 but using your list of the two areas to work on for your group.

5.3 The group has completed the commitment charting exercise described in Chapter 1. Sue has a partime job; she can commit 3 h/week to this PBL course. The other four members all commit to 12 h/week. Resolve how you will handle this.

5.3 What advice would you give Arnie (for the problem that introduced this Chapter)?

5.4 Complete FIRO-B, Jungian typology and Johnson's conflict style inventories. Share the results among group members. Discuss the implications.

5.5 From MPS **28**. Understand what you do in a group. Pair up; one is the client, the other is the observer. With clusters of 5 pairs, ask the 5 clients to sit in a circle and, as a group, take 20 minutes to work on exercise 5.1, 5.2, 5.3 or

5.4. Before the group begins, the 5 observers position themselves outside the circle such that they can see, and hear, their client clearly. While the clients work on the problem, the observers complete (for their client only) the feedback form given in Table 5-1. At the end of the meeting, the group should monitor, as described in Section 5.3-6. Use information from the monitoring session to assist in completing the feedback. Then, the client-observer pairs meet privately to share observations and implications (4 min). Then reverse roles. The clients become observers and vice versa. Repeat the activity on another problem.

6 *What is self-directed, interdependent, small group, problem-based learning?*

Who gives the direction to a small group of students addressing a problem? The tutor, Professor Ego, tells the group:

> "Here are the issues that you must address in this problem of *Arnie's group*."

Compare this with a self-directed learning where the student group members decide the issues that are important to them. In self-directed, interdependent learning, the group does more than agree upon its own objectives. The group assumes responsibility for all eight tasks in PBL, as outlined in Chapter 2 and reproduced here.

Assuming responsibility of these tasks is hard work. Motivation is high; but students are usually ill-prepared to assume the responsibility. As one student wrote in his journal:

> "This topic was too important for the teacher to leave to the students to learn through this SDL approach."

So why do it?

In short, because learning subject knowledge today is not sufficient for the challenges of tomorrow. You will need to keep yourself up-to-date. You will need to learn new knowledge each week of the rest of your life. In addition, in the short run, with training, you will learn the current subject material better **and** you will learn learning skills needed for a lifetime. Knowledge is doubling every five years.

Eight tasks

1. Explore the problem, create hypotheses, identify issues. Elaborate.

2. Identify what you know already that is pertinent.

3. Identify what you do **not** know.

4. As a group, prioritize the learning needs, set learning goals and objectives, and allocate resources, members identify which tasks each will do.

5. Individual self-study and preparation.
6. Return to the group, share the new knowledge effectively so that all the group learn the information.

7. Apply the knowledge to solve the problem.

8. Assess the new knowledge, the problem solution and the effectiveness of the process used. Reflect on the process.

Table 6-1 Comparing teacher-directed with other approaches

	Teacher-directed	Learning on your own	Self-directed independent	Self-directed interdependent
Educational fundamentals of how to learn	Aware of and must use.	Rarely aware of; follow intuition.	Aware of and uses them to help learn for self.	Aware of and must use to learn the subject for self and to teach others.
Issues and objectives,	Considers many issues and selects the pertinent ones, sets objectives explicitly.	Intuitively, but not explicitly, may set objectives. Rarely considers many issues for the subject.	Student explicitly sets objectives, considers many issues that affects subject.	Group considers issues, sets objectives explicitly.
Resources	Asks people for input; considers wide variety of resources, and selects most pertinent.	Usually picks a single book.	Student explores many and selects pertinent ones. Rarely asks advice of people. "Wants to do it on his/her own!"	Draw on people as resources; group considers wide variety of resources.
Difficult topics	Agonizes through difficult concepts and develops alternative ways of "learning them".	For a difficult topic, may give up and "hope that it doesn't matter if I can't understand it all."	Agonizes through difficult concepts.	Agonizes through difficult concepts and develops alternative ways of "teaching them" to the group.
Assessment: criteria, evidence	Creates criteria and selects form of evidence to be supplied.	Considers tests as something to be avoided; rarely sets tests for self. Assumes "I know it".	Student may create self-performance tests to demonstrate for self that the goals have been achieved.	Creates criteria and selects form of evidence to be supplied for both the subject knowledge learned and the <u>process</u> used for learning.
Structure of knowledge and context	Teacher sometimes creates structure and context of the knowledge.	Rarely sees structure and context.	Creates structure to see how/where the new knowledge applies.	Create structure via embedding the new knowledge in the solution to the problem situation.
Relating new knowledge to episodic experience	Plans activities to relate new knowledge to episodic experiences.	Rarely relates.	Sometimes reflects on applications.	

Young professionals will have five career changes in their lifetime; the key need of graduates of colleges and universities is to have lifetime learning skills - these are some of the quotes that emblazon our newspapers. Hence, a major reason why you should become skilled in self-directed, interdependent learning is that *you will acquire learning skills vital to your future success.*

In this Chapter we explore some of options for learning and suggest some advantages and disadvantages for each. The options considered are teacher-directed learning, self-study, self-directed independent learning and self-directed interdependent learning.

6.1 Some Options for Learning

Table 6-1 gives four options for learning and compares how each addresses the issues of applying the fundamentals of learning theory, selecting objectives, picking the text, handling challenging topics and assessing the quality of the learning. Table 6-2 lists issues similar to the eight tasks in PBL or in any learning situation. Some of these relate to the issues listed in Table 6-1. At this time, no indication is given as to who is responsible for doing each task.

In **teacher-directed**, the teacher (or tutor) is responsible for all issues. This would be illustrated in Table 6-2 by an entry in the Left Hand column under tutor for each activity. At present, you might prefer that option. In your career, you will not have instant access to a teacher. You will have to depend on other approaches for lifetime learning.

In **student-directed learning**, the student is responsible for all the activities listed in Table 6-2. This would be shown as entries in the Right Hand column of Table 6-2. Under this general title are three variations. In **self-study**, students usually are unaware of the fundamentals to improve learning and just do what they know to do intuitively. Although motivation is high because they are in charge, the learning may be very effective; or, it may be disaster. The results are usually mixed. Some structure and explicit self-directedness will help. Furthermore, regrettably few "lifetime-learning skills" are acquired.

Two other student-directed options are self-directed, independent learning and self-directed, interdependent learning. Consider each in turn.

6.2 Self-directed, Independent Learning

In self-directed, independent learning, the student takes over all of the activities and depends solely

Table 6-2 Who is responsible for each activity?

Activity	Tutor	Shared	Student
Pick problem			
Identify issues			
Goals/criteria			
Pick resources			
Create assessment			
Do assessment			
Embed knowledge in problem			
Reflect on process			

on him/herself. He/she becomes very sensitive to his/her own learning preference and style.

The advantages of this style are that motivation is high, and that you learn and apply the fundamentals and organizational structure of "lifetime learning skills" to satisfy your own needs. You learn how to look up and assess information. You learn to be independent.

The disadvantages are that you have to learn about "learning", that you need to discipline yourself to create objectives and criteria, to create learning contracts with yourself, and to provide evidence to yourself that you have accomplished your learning goals. All this is well and good. However, the best, most accessible and most efficient way to acquire new information is to **ask someone**. People are the greatest resource of information. A $20 telephone call to the world-authority on a subject can save you thousands of dollars spent trying to ferret the information out of the library. In turn, you are a world-authority in your area of expertise. There is a skill in being able to teach that expertise to others: to anticipate the types of questions they will have, and to sequence your explanations. An interdependence exists. Why not learn those skills in the context of PBL?

A further disadvantage is that self-directed, independent learning skills are insufficient for small group PBL. The independence is contradictory to the group process, to the group selection of the goals and to the group application of problem solving skills to use the learned knowledge to solve the problem.

For the small group PBL format to be effective, team members should be empowered with self-directed, interdependent learning skills.

6.3 Self-directed, Interdependent Learning

In self-directed, interdependent learning, the student group takes over the responsibility. The individuals divide the teaching task and teach and

learn from each other. For example, within any group meeting, Giselle is both a teacher (when she is the expert) and a student (when she seeks to learn from teammate Audrey). She learns to ask probing questions that will improve her learning. She learns to extract knowledge from peers and people so that she doesn't have to consult books. She overcomes the temptation that she *must learn it all for herself*. Frankly, with the rapid expansion of knowledge and the limit of 24 hours in a day, one person can't read it all.

The advantages of this approach is that you learn lifetime learning skills in the context that people are the best resource for information. These **interdependent** "lifetime learning skills" are superior to independent lifetime learning skills.

The disadvantage is that you not only have to learn the information for yourself, but you have to become skilled at communicating and teaching that information to others. It is hard work!

6.4 Making the Most of the Self-directed, Interdependent, Small group, PBL Format

From a learning viewpoint, all research points to the advantage of the PBL format. We learn more, we learn better and the knowledge is integrated and memorized in more accessible and applicable forms. In addition, we are acquiring lifetime learning skills in the context that people are the greatest resource of information. However, to make the most of this approach, we need to reflect on our skill at self-directed, interdependent learning.

6.5 Summary

Self-directed, interdependent learning gives to the group members the responsibility of creating group learning objectives, of developing criteria, of selecting learning resources, of learning some new knowledge and teaching it to other group members, of assessing the degree to which that new knowledge has been learned, of using that knowledge to solve the problem and of reflecting so as to improve the process used in learning and growing together.

Thus, group members are motivated, learn new knowledge more effectively and acquire vital skills in interpersonal relations and in lifetime learning.

6.6 Exercises

6.1 Some of the issues related to learning are challenging to address. For example, defining the learning objectives for a problem or assessing the degree to which you have learned the knowledge. For some of these, you might prefer that the "teacher" or tutor do this. From Table 6-2, which issues are you prepared to accept fully? which ones would you prefer be shared jointly with the tutor? and which ones would you prefer the tutor did?

6.2 Different schools use different versions of PBL. On Table 6-2, draw on a line showing the degree to which each of the issues is handled by: you, the tutor or shared. An

example is given in Table 6-3 for the MPS program.

6.3 Concerning the learning objectives: the teacher/school must ensure that certain knowledge has been learned before a student can "graduate". Some options are that the teacher needs to a) create detailed, specific objectives, b) create global objectives and let the groups decide on detailed, specific objectives for each problem, c) have no objectives; rather the tutor monitors the group objectives and "corrects" these to ensure that the curriculum is covered or d) use some other approach for monitoring objectives. Discuss how this is handled in your program.

6.4 The assessment must be consistent with the objectives. If the group has created the learning objectives, and the tutor assesses the knowledge, how is the consistency between objectives and assessment achieved? After all, the purpose of self-directed learning is to get away from students having to ask "What is going to be on the exam?" How is assessment related to learning objectives for your PBL experience?

Table 6-3 Who is responsible for each activity in the MPS program?

Activity	Tutor	Shared	Student
Pick problem	●		
Identify issues			●
Goals/criteria		●	
Pick resources			●
Create assessment			●
Do assessment			●
Embed knowledge in problem			●
Reflect on process			●

7 Self-directed, interdependent learning skills

Ravinder's group

"I don't understand it. I said I would learn about the effect on platelet abnormality on petechia bleeding. I did! I told you the usual platelet count (150,000 to 400,000 per cc); I know the laboratory tests; the probability that..," On and on Caroline whined.

"Yes," thought Ritchie. "But we still don't have a clue about your topic. You know it; we don't. I'm going to have to pull an all-nighter and learn it for myself by reading Friedman."

"We could follow what you said," ventured Ravinder, "but I didn't learn enough from it."

"Well I learned it; why couldn't you?" responded Caroline bitterly.

Why couldn't you, indeed...

The group has identified meaningful learning objectives. Each accepted responsibility for learning a topic and returning to teach the group that knowledge. That teaching should be so skilled that no group member will feel like Ritchie felt in Ravinder's group. All will feel that they "know" sufficient in that subject. We note in this problem, only Caroline felt she had learned the material.

In small group PBL you will be working in groups as self-directed, interdependent learners.

For this situation, what do you know already about self-directed, interdependent learning?

Perhaps you already are skilled in self-directed, independent learning. What about interdependent learning? You know how to explore issues, create observable objectives that are consistent with measurable criteria. You can identify a rich set of learning resources. You are skilled at learning the information for yourself and working and reworking the information so that you can teach it effectively to others. If you know all of the issues and details for this situation already, skip to the next Chapter.

For this situation, what are the issues?

Some of the issues, for self-directed, interdependent learning, are illustrated in Figure 7-1. In particular, these are:

1. To know and be able to apply the fundamentals of learning, both for independent learning on your own and for interdependent learning.

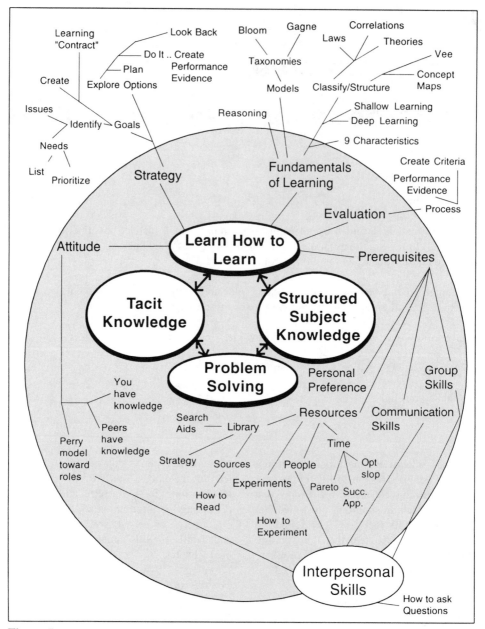

Figure 7-1 Issues in interdependent, self-directed learning

2. To be able to create observable learning objectives/goals that are consistent with measurable criteria that explain the degree to which the goals will be achieved.

3. To be able to identify and locate good resources for the information.

4. To be able to critically (and perhaps creatively) assess the information and to resolve what you believe to be true.

5. To have the patience, initiative and skill to sort out difficult topics.

6. To express your knowledge in a form so that others may learn that knowledge efficiently, effectively and accurately and so that they each have learned all the fundamentals. They might wish to try applying the ideas or working problems.

7. To be skilled at asking questions and at soliciting information from others so that you learn all the fundamentals of a new topic. You do not feel that you have to learn it on your own.

8. To be able to use the combined new knowledge to solve the problem.

9. To value your peers as valid resources of information.

Each of these issues is considered in turn. You may wish to go directly to the section that answers your needs.

7.1. Apply the Fundamentals of Learning

What is learning? How can we improve our learning? How can we help others learn from us?

Learning is not the memorization of a set of isolated ideas. New knowledge is "added" to existing knowledge structures in our Long Term Memory; the structures are "restructured" to create new patterns or to extend and create connection between the new and the old structures. The patterns are "fine tuned" to make them more efficient for different purposes. (Norman as cited in McKeachie, 1978). For example, we might know and can apply ideas about:

- Motivation, self-talk, anger, and time management and are missing a good understanding about "stress". We add new knowledge about "stress" by reading the books by Selye (1975, 1978) and by Michenbaum (1983). This new knowledge "stress" is shown as a square set of knowledge on Figure 7-2a. The previous structure had a circular gap for the new knowledge.

- As we read about stress we realize that this affects motivation, and is affected by our self-talk, time management and our ability to handle anger. Thus, we modify our previously known ideas about these. Our understanding changes on all of these. This is illustrated by the black blob that is embedded into the structure in Figure 7-2b.

- Fine tuning occurs as we realize that this new knowledge alters how we behave in different situations and how we solve problems and how we respond to problems. Thus, the whole structure is fine-tuned, as suggested in Figure 7-2c.

How does one do this?

1. Motivate first. Provide a reason for adding the new knowledge; we should see its usefulness. For example, posing a dilemma to be resolved, a problem to be solved, outlining what you will be able to do with the knowledge gained from the study - these are all ways we can use to motivate the learning (Bird, 1990).

2. Goals. Have them! Goals motivate us (Klausmeier, 1971). Goals improve our performance (Harrisberger, 1974; Stice, 1978; Locke et al., 1981) Create learning objectives or goals. These should be written in words that make the goals "observable".

Goals alone are not enough. To remove ambiguity as to whether we have achieved the goals or not, set measurable criteria that will tell us when the goals have been achieved.

3. **Give the context**: Relate the new knowledge to previous knowledge. Any subject exists in some context. There is a big picture. There are relationships between the new knowledge and past experience (or previous "knowledge structures"). Help the learner see the context.

4. **What?: Select the parts of the new knowledge**: The parts may include: preamble, orientation (where this fits in), definition, key points, proof or evidence substantiating the key points or fundamentals upon which these key points are based, extension of the key points, positive and negative examples, reservations and limitations, relations of the key points to other topics, practical numerical order-of-magnitude values of the phenomena and asides and red herrings. Brown and Atkins (1988) describe some of these. Figure 7-3 summarizes this as a framework to help us select content. If the new knowledge requires reasoned arguments, Paul (1992) outlines another framework shown in Figure 7-4. The situation leads to a selection of the point-of-view or frame of reference. This, in turn, leads to assumptions that lead to concepts and theories that lead to pertinent evidence. Next in the cycle is the interpretation or

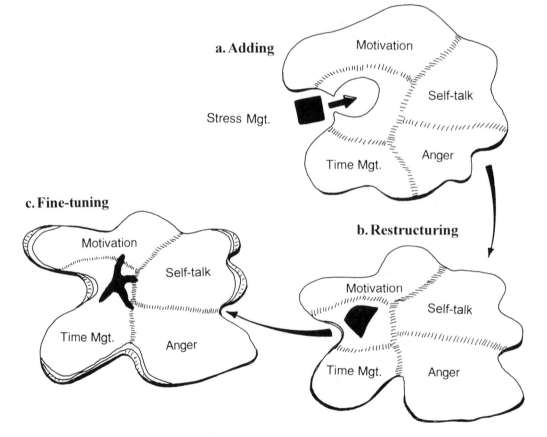

Figure 7-2 Learning by adding new knowledge, restructuring existing knowledge and fine-tuning the structure.

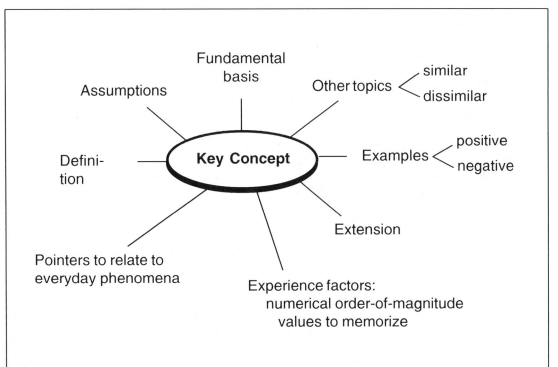

Figure 7-3 Some key points to consider when choosing what to present

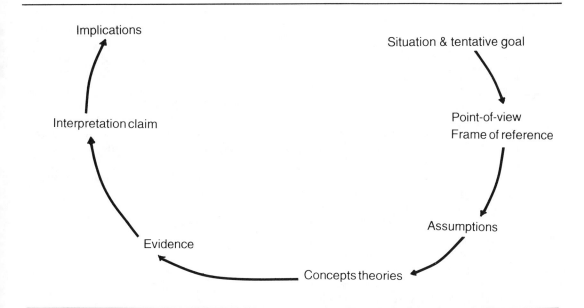

Figure 7-4 Some key points to consider when choosing what to present about reasoned arguments

claim that extends to consequences and implications. Figure 7-3 and 7-4 help us to select **what** needs to be addressed and learned.

5. **Order the presentation: select the sequence:** Sequence the learning: from concrete to abstract; from simple to complex. We think of ideas in different terms. Some prefer to think in abstract terms; others in very concrete. Clement (1978) illustrates this as four internal levels of thinking, illustrated in Figure 7-5. Although we should be able to work at, and shift between, all levels, we should learn progressing from the bottom to the top. A

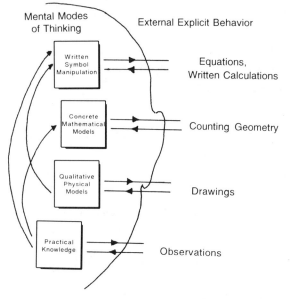

Figure 7-5 Clement's mental modes of thinking (used with permission)

related approach, described in other words, is given by Kolb (1979), Karplus et al. (1990), Piaget et al. (1975) and McCarthy (1980). They talk in terms of a four-stage learning cycle illustrated in Figure 7-6. We experience a concrete event; we reflectively observe and ask "what if?" questions; we gradually create an abstract concept or hypothesis which suggests a practical application. Thus, this particular model suggests that we learn as we convert

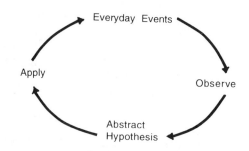

Figure 7-6 The learning cycle

experiences to observations, to abstractions and to actions.

Thus, usually we should:

- *work from the observable to the theoretical.*

Bloom (1956) Krathwohl (1964) and Simpson (1966) suggest that learning be classified into three different domains: thinking, attitudes and tactile or psychomotor. For each of these we should work from simple to complex. For example, for thinking about new knowledge, we mean, start by memorizing a new idea, then comprehending where that new knowledge fits into previously known ideas, applying the knowledge to well-defined situations and then applying the knowledge to successively more difficult tasks of analysis, synthesis and judgement. Thus, the knowledge is learned and then applied to gradually increasingly complex situations. This is summarized in Figure 7-7. Thus, usually we should:

- *start simply.*

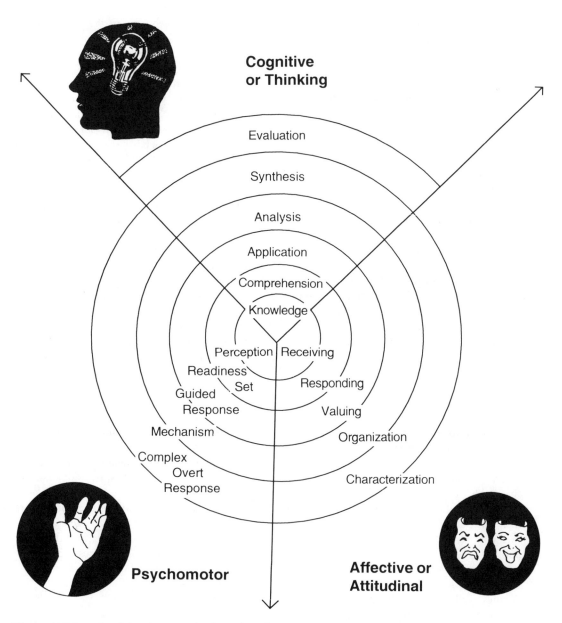

Figure 7-7 Levels of development in three domains

We should match the sequence and form to the preferred style of the learner. Some prefer to think in words; others in pictures and diagrams and still others prefer equations and tables. What is your preferred style? Maybe the key concepts need to be expressed in different forms so that all will understand regardless of his/her preference. Felder and Silverman (1988) and Felder (1990) review five ways in which learners can differ. These are:

- Jungian **S-N** dimension preference: **S** prefers examples and explicit ideas. **N** prefers abstract theories, principles and the big picture.

- Kolb's **Active/reflective** preference: Active prefers to work and process the data. Reflective prefers to think about the information.

- Inductive/deductive preference: Inductive prefers to have data and evidence presented first; then the theory. Deductive prefers the reverse order.

- Visual/auditory preference:

- Serialistic/holistic preference: Serialist prefers material to be presented one-at-a-time with a gradual increase in complexity. Global or holistic prefers the complex, big-picture first. Felder (1990a).

Thus, usually we should target the sequencing and form to

- account for the variety of learning styles of the group members.

In summary, sequence the presentation to work from observable to theoretical, start simply and account for the preferred learning style of your group members.

6. **Planning the presentation: describe the sequence**: The added, new knowledge has different parts: definition, explanation, examples as illustrated in Figure 7-3. Describe the sequence in which the different parts will be considered. "First, we will be an example; then a definition; then an elaboration, etc. " Ausubel (1960) calls these "advance organizers". These help us to see how we are going to be "fed the information".

7. **Account for restructuring:** The issues pertinent to restructuring are a) previously learned misconceptions, b) the importance of deep learning and c) the type of structure for the memorized knowledge that we are trying to create.

a) Misconceptions: Often we may have to first **unlearn** before we can learn. We come to any situation with a host of background ideas and experiences. Some of them are wrong! The polite word is, "we have a misconception". We need to identify the misconception first, and unlearn it before we can acquire the new knowledge.

b) Importance of deep learning. Entwistle (1981) suggests that, although students might display one of six learning "styles" (deep versatile, comprehensive, operational, surface, hard worker and drop out noted in the last column of Table 7-1), we learn best as **deep versatiles**. In this style, learners integrate both the overview and the details and relate these to past personal experience. Unfortunately, even those learners who exhibit the desired "deep processing" attitude and skill will shift to being "surface learners" if they:

- have too much work to do;
- are stressed;
- expect examinations that "test" surface processing and memorization of information;
- are in an environment (instructor, course or department) that rewards surface learning.

In summary, most of us are deep processors. We wish to comprehend, understand, relate the new knowledge (rather than memorize and regurgitate). However, if the pressure becomes excessive or if we see little merit, then we will merely surface process.

Create an environment that
encourages and rewards, and allows sufficient time for "deep" processing.

Another way of viewing "deep processing" is: "Don't try to learn everything from the first activity. Build up your subject knowledge successively. Recall the overall scheme in Figure 2-2."

Table 7-1 Deep processing versus **surface** processing and five other styles

Student's view of the purpose of a university & his/her role.	Student's attitude & fears.	Characteristics of learning style.		Comment	Name of learning style
		At the start of a learning task	Later in the learning task		
University has personal meaning. It supplies resources. I learn..	I am an autonomous, self-learner.	a) Get overview	b) Relates new ideas to personal experience by analogies. c) Identifies the limitations & tests evidence to ensure it supports the conclusions. d) Relates conclusions and evidence to the overview.	Depth understanding.	**Deep versatile**
		a) Get overview	b) Relates new ideas to personal experience by analogies.	Incomplete understanding because of inappropriate analogies used.Have the big picture but not the details	**Comprehensive**
Authorities tell me what to learn and I reproduce it.	I'm afraid of failing. Therefore, I study hard. I study what is in the syllabus.	c) Identifies the limitations & tests evidence to ensure it supports the conclusions.	d) Relates conclusions and evidence to the overview.	Incomplete understanding because it is not put into context through personal experience.	**Operational**
		Memorizes everything.	Overlearns.	Memorized ideas with no relationships.	**Surface**
I want high marks.	I hope for success. I'm confident. I'm stable	Any of the above.		High grades with or without understanding.	**Hard worker. "E" for effort.**
Social life is terrific.					**Drop out.**

c) Knowledge structure: As illustrated in Figure 7-2, new knowledge should be added to appropriate existing structures. This may not happen. In simplistic terms, one can imagine the knowledge being learned as a set of unrelated stuff to be memorized. This "higgeldy piggeldy" structure is illustrated in Figure 7-8. If the information has been selected to facilitate learning, then the structure might be similar to the outline in Figure 7-3. Hopefully, during the "restructuring" and "fine tuning" the structure is honed to facilitate its future use. Glaser (1985) Voss (1985) Reif and Heller (1982)

Higgeldy piggeldy

Structure to facilitate learning; similar to that used in the textbook.

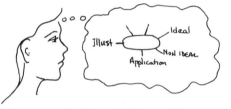

Structure to facilitate problem solving

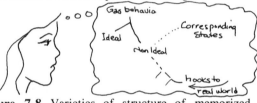

Figure 7-8 Varieties of structure of memorized knowledge

suggest that for problem solving, the facilitating structure is:

a. The knowledge is structured hierarchically, (with fundamental laws and principles at the higher levels and surface structure and pointers at the lower levels).

b. The highest levels in the hierarchy-- or the underpinnings-- are the fundamental laws, the abstractions.

c. The lower levels are the surface structure (or descriptions of the everyday events that work because of the fundamentals) and "pointers" that link the surface structure to the fundamentals. The "pointers" hook the knowledge to the real world.

d. It is organized in blocks convenient for mental processing.

More details are given by Woods and Sawchuk (1993).

Hence, we can try to present the new knowledge in a way to help the creation of this structure. How? By ensuring that we identify the fundamental underpinnings and the assumptions, by giving the "pointers" that relate everyday events to the new ideas and by relating the new knowledge to past experiences.

8. **Facilitate the learning:** be active. Even if someone is talking, make notes. Write it out. Researchers found that we are six times more likely to remember an idea if we write it down.

Various charts, checklists and procedures have been developed to aid the analysis. I recommend the use of Larkin's checklist (1974); Reif's scripts (1986); the Gowin V and the concept map approaches (Novak and Gowin, 1984).

9. **Aid the recall for learners.** Buzan (1975) suggests that retention is aided if the new knowledge is reviewed systematically and periodically after it has been first learned. He recommends that we review the information at the following times: after 10 minutes, 24 hours, 1 week. 1 month, and 6 months.

7.2 Be a Skilled Independent Learner:

Knowles (1975) and Tough et al. (undated) suggest that independent learners plan their learning by addressing the following issues: their needs, learning objectives, learning resources and strategies, types of evidence to show accomplishment and the criteria to decide merit or to validate that the objectives have been achieved.

Table 7-2 An example learning contract summarizing the issues that affect "planned independent learning"

Name: _____*Brian*_____   Subject/skill learned _____*Capital cost estimation*_____

Learning objectives	Learning resources and strategies	Types of evidence to show accomplishment	Criteria to decide on merit; validation
Knowledge *Components in costs* *Inflation indices* *Methods to estimate:* *factor methods* *bare module* *FOB costs from* *correlations* *Alloys: L+M* *Process costs*	*Father* *Chapter 1 in Woods'* *"Cost estimation..."* *Ulrick's book..*	*Recall definitions.* *Look up a data source within 3 min.* *Able to estimate the L+M factor that agrees within ±20% with values from other group members.*	*100% accuracy for definitions.* *Agreement by other group members that value is correct.*
Application *Solve initial problem and* *solve example problems posed by other groups or from "example Company" handout.*		*Can demonstrate process.*	*As individual, compare with sample solutions and have 100% on procedure and 90% on numerical answer.*
Skill *Can apply "Optimum sloppiness" and "successive approximation."*			*Can produce answer **in the time available** and can identify accuracy of answer.*
Attitude *Confidence I can use these skills.*			*Create a "panic scale" and use this to test my reaction to the problem assignments given by peers. Score better than 7 out of 10.*
Value *Importance in profession, ethics and the environment.*		*Can describe to another the value of cost estimation relative to technical competence.*	

These issues can be addressed systematically through a "learning contract". A sample is given in Table 7-2.

Consider some of these issues, in turn.

7.2-1: Create Observable Learning Objectives with Consistent Measurable Criteria

Set goals. Express the objectives in words that describe an "observable" goal. Add measurable criteria that tell us when the goal has been achieved. If you need more information, consult Mager (1962); Kibler et al. (1974) and MPS **3** and **31**.

7.2-2: Identify the Type of Evidence You Would Supply to Show Accomplishment

Having goals and criteria is insufficient. We need to identify the type of evidence that we would produce to show that we have completed the task: journal or diary, project report, verbal presentation, reflective report, statements from peers.

7.2-3: Identify and Locate Probable Learning Resources

Identify clearly in your own mind, what precisely you need: an overview? the latest developments? the relationship of this topic to others? This gives the basis for action. People are your best resource. Learn from an expert. If you search the literature, consult the reference librarian. Provide a precise definition of what you are looking for.

For more, see Chapters 6 and 7 in Marshall and Rowland (1981).

7.2-4: Use the Tutor as a Resource for Subject Knowledge

de Grave et al. (1990) and Dolmans et al. (1993) reported that for groups having faculty tutors, students inherently counted on the tutor to elaboratively explain subject content. On the other extreme, when our student groups are empowered to function without a tutor, our experience has been that the student groups **did not** call on the tutor (available in the room) for advice for subject knowledge. They did not use the tutor as a resource. They try to do it themselves. It's as if they are trying to prove that they can "do it alone".

My advice is not to overlook the tutor as a resource for subject knowledge. Use the tutor as a resource!

7.2-5: Assess the Information

Critically appraise the information. Sort out what you believe. Marshall and Rowland (1981) offer good introductory advice (with emphasis on reading books). In general, be critical. Read anything with the hope that the author's conclusions are valid but with a healthy pessimism that says "**prove it** to me". Check the author's point-of-view, assumptions, data and evidence presented and reasoning used to reach conclusions. Be unwilling to accept the conclusions unless all these components are handled well.

Specific suggestions about how to read and critically analyze what we read depend on the type of literature and the purpose. For scientific journal articles, a general strategy is skim read, understand and check.

Skim read the title, abstract, conclusion and then the introduction. The title suggest what the author thought the work was about. The abstract and conclusions provide more details. The introduction puts it into context. Then, very briefly skim read the theory and experimental approach. From this you should be able to:
- state what the article is about;
- define the problem the author is attempting to solve;
- give an impression of what the author claims to have done.

This completes the skimming stage.

Now *understand it*. Concentrate now on the theory, experimental approach, point-of-view and assumptions, results, discussion and conclusions. Some of these may not be stated explicitly. (In particular, the weakest sections are usually the "point-of-view", the "discussion" where the author rarely does a good job of putting his/her research in the context of previous work, and the "conclusions" where the author does not draw a rich enough set of conclusions from his/her study.) Search for clear and consistent definitions, and for clear identifications as to who says what and who believes what. Separate "measured data" from "data-calculated-from-the-measurements".

Next, check to *determine the facts and evaluate the conclusions*. Are the conclusions valid? What facts can you draw? Check the theory, experimental section. Are they consistent? Does the experiment really test the theory? Check sampling methods, statistical workup of the data, biases, consistency checks. What conclusion can you draw?

Huck and Sandler (1979) list 20 threats to internal validity of conclusions. For medical students, a series of papers by Sackett et al. (1981) describe how to critically appraise the clinical literature.

7.3 Be a Skilled Interdependent Learner

Interdependent learners attend to all of the tasks done by independent learners. In addition, they do many of these tasks cooperatively that provides a supportive climate for each other. Interdependent learners should also provide opportunity for reflection about their learning. Here are four additional suggestions to improve your interdependent effectiveness.

7.3-1: Help others: Work in the Context of the Independent Learning of Others

If you find information that is pertinent to others, then let them know share this information. You are working together. This means that before your group disbands, everyone must know what the others are working on. Know how to contact them. Get information to them that will help their independent learning.

7.3-2: Learning the Information for Yourself is Not Enough: Anticipate the Learning Needs of the Group Members

Learning the information for yourself is not enough. You need to think of the different learning needs the members of your group. Ask yourself the question, "How does Becky learn best?" and then express the new ideas in that form. Draw on the knowledge about teaching, some of which was given in Section 7-1.

7.3-3: Think of the Mechanics of Your Teach Meeting

As you prepare for the teach meeting, begin to appreciate its complexity and the length of time you might need to teach others. Think about the form of presentation and the time available. Explore with the chairperson of the "teach meeting" to agree on the place in the agenda and the time available. You might have discussed previously, in the goals meeting, the preferred style and amount of time available.

7.3-4: Anticipate the Questions You Need Answered from the Other Member's Contributions

The "teach meeting" is for you to learn too. Come to learn. Think about the questions you have. How does the information that the others prepare relate to what you know? What do you need to know?

7.4 Put it All Together: the Teach Meetings

Many options are available. The group may decide that each will learn **the same** subject. The group meeting will be to hear the different perspectives and to sort it out. The group may decide that each will learn a **different** subject. Everyone will rely the others to be the "sole" source of information. Your group may decide something else.

The suggestions given here are for a teach meeting where each brings a different set of knowledge he/she has learned.

7.4-1: Come prepared

Bring your handouts and demonstrations; bring material you need to learn. Be on time.

7.4-2: Come to share

Everytime I start a new course in the fall, I'm a little nervous. And I have been an educator for over 30 years. Expect to be a little nervous.

Next, focus on an attitude of "sharing" (not "telling em'") what you know. You can unwittingly increase your nervousness by coming with the attitude that you are to tell them everything they need to know. What an awesome responsibility you place on your shoulders! Using the tellin attitude will make you too nervous. "Do I know it all? What if they know more than I do on this subject?" Focus, instead, on sharing the knowledge you have as best you can.

This attitude helps us also when we are questioned. Questions tend to make us defensive if our attitude is "we have to tell em; I've got to be the expert". On the other hand, questions help our learning if our attitude is one of sharing.

7.4-3: Come to learn

Yes, you come to the meeting to share the knowledge you have learned. But, you also need to learn the knowledge presented by others. Come ready to learn from them.

7.4-4: Understand the Role of the Tutor

What is the role of the tutor in your group? chairperson? referee to sort out competing ideas? subject expert? Clarify the role of the tutor.

7.5 Summary and How to Monitor and Give Feedback

In self-directed learning you assume all the characteristics of the teacher. You take control of your own learning. You set goals and criteria. You decide on the types of evidence you would use to show growth. You relate the knowledge to the problem that drives the learning.

In a group setting and working as a team, you work interdependently. That is, you work as a group to decide on goals and objectives. You learn independently some new knowledge that will benefit both you and the group. You teach that knowledge to the other members of the group. Likewise, they teach you. You learn to rely on

them. You see them as valid and valued sources of information. You learn to ask questions so as to learn from them.

Table 7-3 gives a feedback form that can help you reflect on, monitor and set goals for growth.

7.6 References

Ausubel, D.P. (1960, 1968) "Educational Psychology: a cognitive view," Holt Rinehart and Winston, New York, NY.

Bird, R.B. (1980) personal communication, University of Wisconsin, Madison, WI.

Bloom, B.S. (1956) "Taxonomy of Educational Objectives: Classification of Educational Goals: Handbook I: Cognitive Domain," McKay, New York. NY.

Brown, G. and M. Atkins (1988) "Effective Teaching in Higher Education," Methuen, London, UK.

Buzan, T. (1975) "Use Your Head," BBC Publication, London, UK.

Clement, J.J. (1978) "Formula-centered knowledge versus conceptual-centered understanding in Physics," Technical Report, Department of Physics, University of Massachusetts, Amherst, MA.

de Grave, W.S., M.L. de Volder, W.H. Gijsaelers and V. Damoiseaux (1990) "Peer Teaching and Problem-based Learning: tutor characteristics, tutor functioning, group functioning and student achievement," in "Innovation in Medical Education: an evaluation of its present status," A.M. Nooman, H.G. Schmidt and E.S. Ezzat, eds., Springer Publishing, New York, 123-134.

Dolmans, D., I. Wolfhagen and H.G. Schmidt (1993) "Validation of a Rating Scale for Tutor Evaluation in a Problem-based Medical Curriculum," Paper presented at the annual meeting

Table 7-3 Feedback for interdependent, self-directed learning

Feedback to _____ for Unit _____ Date _____

Present & on time: ☐   Present but late by _____ min.   Absent ☐

Quality of Knowledge: good intellectual understanding of the topic, the material supplied was complete and appropriate.

None of these.	A few but major omissions.		Most of these.		All of these.
O_____O_____O_____	_____O_____	_____O_____	_____O_____	_____O

Quality of Instruction: he/she was here on time, the presentation was focused on the new knowledge; good choice of material and medium with effective communication and resource material supplied.

None of these.	A few but major omissions.		Most of these.		All of these.
O_____O_____O_____	_____O_____	_____O_____	_____O_____	_____O

Followup: from this presentation I will have to:

Must study subject on my own; I learned nothing from your presentation.	Major self-study needed. I have some starting references from your presentation.	Some self-study of the basics.		No self-study of the basics. I want to reflect about the ideas.
O_____	_____O_____	_____O_____	_____O_____	_____O_____	_____O

Strengths   Areas to Improve on

_____   _____

_____   _____

_____

_____

_____

_____   from D.R. Woods, "How to Gain the Most from PBL," (1994)

of the American Educational Research Association, Atlanta, GA, April.

Entwistle, N. (1981) "Styles of Learning and teaching," John Wiley and Sons, New York, NY.

Felder, R.M. (1990a) "Meet your Students: Susan and Glenda," Chem. Eng. Ed., **24**, 1, 7 and 11.

Felder, R.M. (1990b) "Meet your Students: Michelle, Rob and Art," Chem. Eng. Ed., **24**, 2, 130-131.

Felder, R.M. and L. Silverman (1988) "Learning and Teaching Styles in Engineering Education," Engineering Education **78**, 7, 674-681.

Friedman, H.H. (1987) "Problem-oriented Medical Diagnosis," A Little, Brown Manual, Little, Brown and Co., Boston, MA.

Glaser, R. (1984) "The Role of Knowledge," American Psychologist **39**, 2, 93-104.

Harrisberger, L. (1974) "Individualized Learning Management: a workshop," University of Guelph, Guelph, ON.

Huck, S.W. and H.M. Sandler (1979) "Rival Hypotheses: alternative interpretations of data based conclusions," Harper & Row Publishers, New York, NY.

Johnson, S.R., and R.B. Johnson (1970) "Developing Individualized Instruction Material," Westinghouse Learning Press, Palo Alto, CA.

Karplus, R. et al. (1980) "Science Teaching and a Development of Reasoning: a workshop," Lawrence Hall of Science, University of California, Berkeley, CA.

Kibler, R.J. et al. (1974) "Objectives for Instruction and Evaluation," Allyn and Bacon, Inc., Boston, MA.

Klausmeier, H.J. et al. (1971) "Learning and Human Abilities: educational psychology," 4th edition, Harper and Row, New York, NY.

Knowles, M. (1964) "Self-directed Learning," Follett Publishing, Chicago, IL.

Kolb, D.A., I.M. Rubin and J.M. McIntyre (1979) "Organizational Psychology: an experiential approach," 3rd ed., Prentice-Hall, Englewood Cliffs, NJ.

Krathwohl, D.R., et al. (1964) "Taxonomy of Educational Objectives: Classification of Educational Goals: Handbook II: Affective Domain," McKay, New York, NY.

Larkin, J.H. (1975) "Developing Useful Instruction in General Thinking Skills," Paper JL010276, Group in Science and Mathematics Education, University of California, Berkeley, CA. Sept.

Locke, E.A., K.N. Shaw, L.M. Saari and G.P. Latham (1981) "Goal Setting and Task Performance: 1969-1980," Psychological Bulletin, **90**, a, 125-152.

Mager, R.F. (1962) "Preparing Educational Objectives," Fearon Publishers, San Francisco, CA.

Marshall, L.A. and F. Rowland (1981) "A Guide to Learning Independently," Longman Cheshire, Melbourne, Australia.

McCarthy, B. (1980) "The 4Mat System," EXCEL, Inc., 600 Enterprise Drive, Suite 101, Oak Brook, IL

McKeachie, W.J. (1978) "Teaching Tips: a guidebook for the beginning college teacher," 7th ed., Heath and Co., Lexington, MA.

Novak, J.D. and D.B. Gowin (1984) "Learning how to Learn," Cambridge University Press, Cambridge, UK.

Paul, R. (1992) "Critical Thinking: what every person needs to survive in a rapidly changing world," 2nd ed., Foundation for Critical Thinking, Santa Rosa, CA.

Piaget, J. and B. Inhelder (1975) "The Psychology of the Child," Basic Books, New York, NY.

Reif, F. and J.I. Heller (1982) "Knowledge Structure and Problem Solving in Physics," Educational Psychologist, **17**, 102-127.

Reif, F. (1986) "Interpretation of Scientific or Mathematical Concepts: Cognitive Issues and Instructional Implications," Paper CES-1, Department of Physics, University of California, Berkeley, CA.

Sackett, D.L., R.B. Haynes, (1981) eight paper series in the Canadian Medical Association Journal, **124**, March, 703; April, 985.

Simpson, E.J. (1966) "Classification of Educational Objectives: Psychomotor Domain," Project Report, University of Illinois; reported by Johnson and Johnson (1970).

Stice, J. (1978) paper presented at the AIChE Annual Meeting, Nov., San Francisco, CA

Tough, A., G. Griffin, Bill Barnard and D. Brundage, (undated) "The Design of Self-directed Learning," videotape and manual, Ontario Institute for Studies in Education, Toronto, ON.

Voss, J. (undated) "Problem Solving and the Educational Process," in "Handbook of Psychology and Education," R. Glaser and A. Lesgold, eds., Lawrence Erlbaum Publishers, Hillsdale, NJ.

Woods, D.R. and R.J. Sawchuk (1993) "Fundamentals of Chemical Engineering Education," Chem. Eng. Ed., Spring, 80-85.

7.7 Exercises.

7.1 For Ravinder's Group, how might the group address this issue?

7.2 Write out the principles you use to prepare the "teaching session" about your topic; contrast this with the approach you would use if you "reported back" to your group about the topic.

8 *What is self-assessed, self-directed, interdependent, small group, problem-based learning?*

Who assesses the learning?
The tutor, Professor Standards, explains:

> "I must do the assessment. After all, I am responsible for knowing whether the students pass or fail."

Compare this with a self-assessed group. Here the group assesses their progress; the tutor assesses the group's assessment process. The tutor considers the quality of the objectives, the consistency of the criteria and the quality of the evidence.

Upon first being given the authority to self-assess, students are tempted to say, "Hurrah, now I can give myself 100." When they acquire the objective skill, they soon learn that usually they are their own severest critics. They discover the challenge of providing evidence that is observable and measurable.

In this Chapter we look at assessment, its role and how it interacts with the self-directed, interdependent, small group PBL activity. Advantages and disadvantages are explored.

8.1 What is Self-assessed, Self-directed, Interdependent, Small Group PBL?

Assessment. What is it? How does self-assessment differ so much from assessment by others? What is the role of self-assessment in PBL?

8.1-1 What is Assessment?

Assessment is judgement. We judge the worthiness of a performance, a creation and an act. Although assessment and judgement are natural, usually we are frightened by and uneasy with assessment. We may

- Equate assessment with "exams"; exams that we find threatening. Alpert and Haber (1960) developed the Anxiety Achievement Test; our results showed that students with high anxiety, as measured by this test, performed lower on examinations than expected. And vice versa.

- Prefer that someone else do the assessment because then, if we can figure out what **they** are testing, we only have to study **that.**

- Incorrectly view it as evil: as something to be dreaded and avoided.

- Incorrectly equate an assessment of performance (or lack of performance) with an assessment of our own personal worth. Assessment is **not** a judgement of personal worth. (Recall from Chapter 1, Perry (1970) found it common for first year University students to incorrectly equate personal value with the marks they received. Some have difficulty changing this attitude.)

To understand more about assessment (and the key components) meet Ted, in Example 8-1.

Example 8-1: Ted's golf game.

Yesterday Ted's score was 85 for 18 holes. He was particularly frustrated because on the #12, par 3, hole he had 7. Everything went wrong on that hole. He usually has par 3 or a bogie 4; occasionally he has had an eagle 2. Today Ted wants to improve his game. He wants particularly to improve his performance on #12. He wants par.

Here, golfer Ted sets a goal "to improve my game today." This is noteworthy. He explicitly set a goal. He could have said, "I'll just play some golf today." Nothing explicit. Let's just go out and do something.
Point #1:

Set explicit goals; you will perform better because of them. Goals help focus your energies. Goals motivate us.

The goal is not stated very well. For example, at the end of the round of golf, Ted could say, "I improved today," even though his score today was 95 whereas yesterday it was 85. Naturally, we would expect improvement to mean **his score improves**. Ted might have meant that he kept his head down more times today than yesterday. He could claim his game improved today because he played around with friendlier people; he enjoyed himself more. To remove the ambiguity, he should have stated his goal less ambiguously and added some measurable criteria. He could have said, "My goal is to improve today; I measure that improvement by having a par 3 on #12 hole." The words "having a par 3 on #12 hole" give the criterion for success.
Point #2:

Include measurable criteria.

Ted set his target at a par 3. He could have set it at a "hole-in-one". But, he has never had a hole-in-one before. He could have set his target at bogie 4. The target should be challenging but achievable.
Point #3:

The goal and the criteria should be achievable with the resources available.

Finally, Ted needs to keep score, especially on hole #12. He needs to supply evidence; usually the evidence would be the score card. If there was a lot at stake, we might insist that an independent observer would count stokes and keep the score card.
Point #4:

There must be agreement as to what constitutes evidence and an effort to collect evidence that satisfies the goal and the criteria.

I hope that this example has helped to show that assessment, itself, is not that frightening. Perhaps, the way the process has been applied in the past has not been the best. Perhaps, it is a challenging task to create goals and criteria consistent with the resources and to select forms of evidence, but as a process, it is pretty straightforward. I hope that we can shift our attitude toward assessment to one of:

>   - ***Assessment helps us improve and grow; without assessment we stagnate.***
>
>   - ***Assessment gives us a sense of accomplishment; we have evidence that we achieved our goals.***
>
>   - ***Assessment removes uncertainty; we have evidence as to the degree to which we have achieved our goal.***

Assessment is vital for growth, motivation and progress.

8.1-2 What is Self-assessment?

Self-assessment is an assessment done by oneself. If someone else does the assessment, then we are always trying to figure out "what *they* want." We act to satisfy them. If they say, "This subject is important and it's going to be on the test," then we study that material. Not because we necessarily want to; rather, because we will be rewarded if we do. We will be penalized if we don't.

Self-assessment gives us full responsibility for the whole assessment process. Being in charge of the assessment processes closes our personal voyage in the self-directed learning cycle of:

>   set goals, create criteria, gather evidence and *apply criteria to demonstrate that the goals have been achieved.*

Self-assessment helps us focus on our task.

Self-assessment motivates the learning process.

As Graham Gibbs (undated) and Joe Novak (1989) point out,

"Whoever owns the assessment owns the learning."

For example, if I set the final exam, then most students are not interested in learning topics because they are interested. Rather, they want to know "Is this going to be on the final?" They devote most of their time trying to identify "What's on the final?" "What are **you** going to test?"

In summary, self-assessment is a natural, if not essential, component to self-directed learning.

8.1-3 Self-assessment in the Context of Self-directed, Interdependent, Small Group PBL

Self-assessment should be used to assess the learning. But the learning of what? I think it can be used effectively to assess the learning of:
   - the subject knowledge,
   - the problem solving skills used,
   - the group process used,
   - the chairperson skills displayed,
   - the acquisition of self-directed, interdependent, lifetime learning.

Whatever knowledge, skills and attitudes you want to develop, their acquisition should be self-assessed.

Having the power to self-assess is not the same as giving students licence to award themselves any mark they wish. Empowerment is matched with accountability. To understand this, let's pause to hear Professor Standards' reaction to self-assessment.

>   "Heresy! What about standards?" exclaims a shocked Professor Standards.

What is the role of the teacher or tutor? The tutor/professor must set and maintain standards and encourage students to achieve and surpass those standards. The tutor has the crucial role of:

>   - Monitoring the quality of the goals. For example, if golfer Ted set a goal to achieve a score of 12 on hole #12, Ted's goals are too low. He should be "failed". Better still, he should be required to set more challenging goals.

- Monitoring the quality and consistency of the measurable criteria. Criteria are difficult to create. Indeed, much of the tutor's role is to help the students acquire skill in creating criteria.

- Monitoring the quality of the evidence the student provides.

- Monitoring the assessment process used by the student and giving feedback on the quality of that activity.

The tutor has the crucial role of maintaining standards by monitoring the self-assessment processes used by the students.

8.2 Advantages and Disadvantages to Being Empowered to Do the Assessment

From a learning viewpoint, all research points to the advantage of self-assessment. It is a natural outcome of the PBL format: it completes the loop in the learning cycle. We learn more, we learn better and the knowledge is integrated and memorized in more accessible and applicable forms. We increase our self-image and self-confidence. In addition, we are acquiring skills in "performance review" that we will need in our working life.

The disadvantages are that it is hard work for both the students and the teacher. For students, our ten years of experience in the MPS program has shown that acquiring confidence in skill in self-assessment seems to be most difficult (Woods et al., 1988). It takes patience, practice, hard work and patient coaching.

The other disadvantage is that the teachers in the PBL program, or in any program, find empowering you with this responsibility is threatening. It takes power from them. It demands more of them because they need to make explicit the assessment process they may have used implicitly for years. It demands more because they need to ensure their standards are reached but from the viewpoint of

monitoring and assessing your student assessment process. Teachers shift from being the assessors of subject content to assessors of your assessment process.

I elaborated on the teacher's viewpoint because both students and teachers need to work together to gain the most from this activity. Both need to value each other's viewpoint and, in particular, to work to overcome the uneasiness each feels as they venture into student self-assessment. This is new territory for both.

8.3 Making the Most of Self-assessed, Self-directed, Interdependent, Small Group PBL

Your particular PBL program may not include the self-assessment component. If it does not, then I would encourage you, on your own, to assess your progress. Learn and apply the assessment process. Compare your process and results with those of peers and tutors. Gradually develop your confidence with self-assessment.

If you are fortunate enough to have self-assessment included in your PBL, be patient with yourself. The attitudes and skills are challenging to acquire. Seek feedback often. Be systematic. Approach self-assessment as a process skill that you are learning. Treat it with the same rigor and approach that you would if you are learning a new concept in Biology.

Enjoy.

8.4 Summary

Self-assessment is challenging. Self-assessment means you are responsible for objectively setting goals, creating criteria, providing evidence and making an objective judgement as to the degree to which the goals have be achieved and the criteria satisfied. The goals should be achievable; not ridiculously easy nor unattainable. The criteria must be measurable and consistent with the goal. We have to be able to see that we have achieved the goals. Wishful thinking is not rewarded here. Evidence must be supplied.

Self-assessment is one of the most powerful educational tools available. Being challenged to set personal learning goals motivates and focuses our energies. Having skills in the assessment process puts us at an enviable advantage for life. Few are comfortable having to assess others.

Acquiring objectivity and confidence in "doing an assessment" is challenging, and is helped by having tutors who shift their role from being the assessor of the *subject matter you are learning* to being the assessors (and coach) of the *process you use in your self-assessment*.

8.5 References

Alper, R. R.N. Haber (1960) J. of Abnormal and Social Psychology **61**, 2, 207-215.

Gibbs, Graham (undated) "An A to Z of Student Focused Teaching Strategies," Oxford Polytechnic, Headington, Oxford, UK.

Novak, Joe (1989) "Teaching in Science and mathematics," Santiago de Compostela, Spain, Sept.

Woods, D.R., R.R. Marshall and A.N. Hrymak (1988) "Self-assessment in the Context of the McMaster Problem Solving Programme," Assessment and Evaluation in Higher Education, **13**, 2, 107-127.

8.6 Exercises

8.1 On a scale from 0 (low) to 10 (high),
- how comfortable are you with the idea of assessing yourself?
- how aware are you of the process you use?
- how skilled (accurate) are you?
Discuss your response with other group members.

8.2 If you wanted to "test the waters" by doing some self-assessment within your PBL group, what would you suggest?

8.3 At the end of a group session, such as described in Chapter 5, each person identifies what they think they contributed to the group. Jeff interrupted, was unprepared and said several racist comments that really rankled you. Now it's Jeff's turn to summarize his contributions to the group. He says, "I was supportive; I contributed new knowledge that helped us move forward on this case when I recalled the events last week in my dorm. I see my main contributions in the morale of the group." You are stunned. You saw evidence that contradicted everything he just uttered. What do you do?

8.4 For the self-assessment in your PBL group, each reflects on the published goals and criteria, completes evidence sheets, reaches an assessment and then privately discusses these with the tutor in his/her office. For "skill in self-directed learning" you rated yourself as being able to demonstrate "most of the goals" (on a scale ranging from "none," "some," "most" and "all"). As you bring out your evidence, the tutor says, "I see you as "some" of the goals." The tutor closes out the situation by saying, "I hope you will do better next time." Comment on this scenario.

9 *Self-assessment skills*

Piet's dilemma

Piet "thinks" that he knows the pertinent knowledge, and how to apply it, to the case of Fluky Phil. But he is unsure.

Piet should be able to decide if he knows the subject. In the past, he has depended on an instructor to give him an exam, or to look over his work and tell him whether he has "passed" or not. The whole process of "self-assessment" happens intuitively for Piet. Indeed, sometimes, in the past, he thought he knew the subject, only to find that he couldn't do the exam. "The exam wasn't what I expected!" exclaimed Piet.

Now in the self-assessed, small group activity, Piet (and you) will be expected to accurately assess your accomplishments. By accurate we mean that other objective observers will agree with your assessment. You will neither overestimate your ability; nor will you underestimate. You will be "right on."

In self-assessed, self-directed, interdependent, small group PBL you will be expected to accurately and objectively self-assess your performance.

For this situation, what do you know already about self-assessment?

Perhaps you already are skilled in self-assessing your abilities and your performance. To decide if you achieved something (whether it is like Piet and the case of Fluky Phil or it is your ability to ski) requires the application of a process, a procedure, a set of conditions. Five components must be addressed in that assessment process:

1) What content is being assessed? Is it Piet's ability to solve the case? to ask questions? to recall facts? to identify issues in the case? to interact "well" with other students in the group? Who decides this?

2) There must be a well-stated, unambiguous goal (what exactly is Piet expecting that he "know"? Piet's first mistake is that he used the ambiguous term "know.") Who creates the goals?

3) Published, measurable criteria identifying the extent to which the goal is achieved ("know" 80%? 100%?) are needed. Who creates the criteria?

Table 9-1 Issues in assessment (based on Alverno College, 1985)

Issues	Details	Options
Goals	Content: what is being assessed?	first law of thermodynamics? Newton's second law? PS?, interpersonal skill? ethics? listening skills? a **product** or the **process** we used to produce a product?
	Observable goals/objectives?	first law of thermodynamics -> "Given.., you will be able to..."
	Who creates the goals?	students? students with input from tutor? tutor? faculty committee? professional licensing agency?
	Explicit and published?	The goals, criteria and assessment **must** all be consistent. Must be explicit and published so no ambiguity exists for either students or assessor.
Criteria	Are they measurable and tied to goals/objectives?	measurable standards with designations as to the variation in and meaning of the grade: A, B? pass/fail?
	Created by?	students? students with input from tutor? tutor? faculty committee? professional licensing agency?
	Explicit and published?	The goals, criteria and assessment **must** all be consistent. All involved, the students and the assessor must be participating on the same field. Hence, the goals and the criteria must be explicit and published so that there is no ambiguity as to what is expected.
Form of evidence	Explicit description given? type of evidence expected that student will supply? What constitutes evidence?	written answer? written answer and the details of how you arrived at the answer? journal of activities? reflective journal? project report? statements from peers? tick marks on an evidence form completed each day? each week?
Student Resources	Consistent with goals & criteria? Reasonable to achieve these goals in the time available?	Having set the goals and the criteria, is it physically and emotionally possible to achieve those goals in the time and resources available? If not, revise goals and criteria.
Assessment process	Purpose of the assessment	check if teacher doing job? provide feedback to student? develop the student's appraisal skill? help student develop self image? provide mark? for certification? force students to reflect & review? provide a mark for grad school? develop student autonomy?
	Performance conditions	take home, hand in 1 week later? three hour exam in classroom? in small group on one side of a one-way mirror?
	Who assesses?	students? students with input from tutor? tutor? faculty committee? professional licensing agency? trained assessors?
	Feedback: form for and type	checklists? rating forms? marking scheme? anecdotal comments? five positives and two areas to work on?
	Feedback: timing, when?	promptly? within 1 week? never?
	Feedback: by whom?	letter? posted on display board? interview with independent tutor? with mentor?
	Training in the assessment process?	is training supplied? how explicit? how detailed? consistency checks done? practice activities with feedback to the assessors? Are the assessors assessed?

4) The time and resources available should be sufficient to make it possible for one to achieve the goal.

5) Some form of evidence has been supplied (such as, answers to a question, or a diagram showing behaviour).

Seven other issues that should be resolved. These include such things as what is the purpose of the assessment? what are the conditions for performance? If you know all the issues and details already skip to the next Chapter.

For this situation, what are the issues?

Some of the issues are summarized in Table 9-1. In particular, these are (and this repeats, for emphasis, the five listed above):

1. What content?

2. What observable goals?

3. What criteria?

4. What resources are available to achieve the goals?

5. What evidence is expected? and

for the process:

6. What is the purpose of the assessment?

7. What are the conditions under which the assessment is done?

8. Who does the assessment?

9. What forms or checklists does the assessor use to make the assessment?

10. When are the results of the assessment given to the student?

11. What are the conditions under which that assessment is given?

12. What training and monitoring are provided for the assessment process?

So many issues! Yet, they all make sense.

Each of these issues is considered in turn. You may wish to go directly to the section that answers your needs.

9-1 What Content?

What is the subject, topic or skill being assessed?

- Which cognitive subject domain? principles of biochemistry, physics, behavioral psychology or social work? In Chapter 2 and the Case of the Dinged Sign, Figure 2-2 listed six "subjects." For these subjects, what level of subject knowledge is expected? Bloom's taxonomy, from Figure 7-7, illustrates six levels.

- For the subject domain, are we expected to memorize numerical values for the experience knowledge? What is a reasonable value for a haematocrit for a healthy 4 year old male? Are the values different for a 65 year old female?

- Which attitudinal dimensions are being assessed? confidence? motivation? ethics?

- Are psychomotor skills important? how to take the blood pressure? withdraw a sample of blood? shake hands? titrate?

- Should problem solving skills be assessed? trouble shooting? clinical problem solving?

- What about interpersonal skills? communication, empathy.

Table 9-2 provides a checklist. Table 9-3 gives an illustrative example for Unit 1 of the McMaster Medical School Program.

Table 9-2 A checklist for "content"

Subject:	Expected level of development					
	Memorize	Comprehend	Apply	Analyze	Synthesize	Evaluate
Knowledge						
Experience knowledge						
Psychomotor skill						
Attitude: confidence; value						
Problem solving						
Interpersonal skills						
Group skills/ chairperson						
Self-directed learning						
Self-assessment						
Professional ethics						
Other						

Within the context of an established program, the faculty would usually create the broad-brush outline of these. Nevertheless, their outline might be very restrictive. In Table 9-2, for example, they might only include the subject knowledge. From your perspective, you might wish to add (and self-assess) other subjects, such as interpersonal skills. Indeed, in PBL, initially many students focus on just the "subject" knowledge. They forget to focus on the process used, the change in attitude, their ability to cope effectively with change, and the group process skills that they are applying. Yet you might want to consider these valued subject knowledge, the acquisition of which should be assessed.

If you don't assess it, you don't know if you've got it!

9-2 What Observable Goals?
Now that the subject has been identified, we should create unambiguous, observable and achievable goals.

Table 9-3 Example subject knowledge to be assessed in the McMaster Medical School Program (Unit 1) (reproduced with permission)

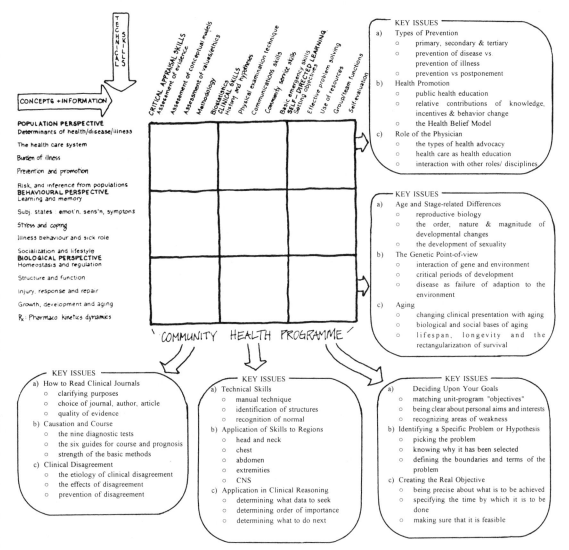

9.2-1 Unambiguous and Observable

If we are going to be able to monitor progress and see accomplishment, then we have to be able to **see** the results being achieved. Hence, the goals and

objectives must be written in "observable terms." For example, it is easy to say that I know the fundamentals of nutrition. But what does this mean? How could I unambiguously show someone (or show myself) that I "know" it. The word

Table 9-4 Is the goal stated unambiguously and in observable words?

Initial goal statement	Comment	Possible Improvement
When I'm finished with this PBL unit: Goren says, "I will know the difference between a circle and an ellipse."	What would you supply as evidence that you "know" the difference? What information would you expect to be given? What would you do with that information?	"Given sketches of a variety of circles and ellipses, I will be able to point to the circles and point to the ellipses."
Maria says, "I will learn everything about normal blood and teach it to the group."	Blood flow? chemicals present? usual values in healthy people of different ages, chemical composition, what it looks like under a microscope?	"Given the age and sex of a healthy human, I will be able to list ten most common chemicals present in blood and the usual range in concentration."
Andre says, "I am good at listing the issues that are important in a problem given to us in PBL."	Terrific, but I don't know what you mean by "good". Here, we might try to address how we would judge "good". Thus, we might combine an observable task with some criterion to judge the goodness of the results.	"Given a problem, I will write down four issues for each of seven different perspectives (and these shall be judged to be valid and comprehensive by the tutor 60% of the time)."

"know" does not describe an observable act; it describes something internal and unobservable. Hence, any goal statement needs to be changed into wording that is unambiguous and observable. The examples in Table 9-4 illustrate the importance of specifying the *given conditions*, and of bringing in *criteria* and a judging process to clarify when we would know that the goal has been achieved. This process is frustrating. In the first column, it is easy for us to describe all that we are going to do "in simple words": "I'm going to learn about blood." However, to remove ambiguity as to what *precisely* is being learned about blood, we have to write out details of, what some call, ridiculous trivia about what is to be done. True. And without that apparent trivia, confusion reigns in the assessment.

Some general steps for creating goals are as follows:

1. State the "content." You might prefer to be very general, at first. Then, list the content area. For example: "biochemistry: reactions of amino acids."

2. Restate the "content" in the form of a goal, learning objective or a "reasonably precise statement about what you expect to "know" or do." Again you can start very generally, "reaction of amino acids." Then make it more specific "What exactly do you need to know about amino acids and their reactions?" "A memorized list of? being able to balance? being able to predict the rate of reaction? listing the factors that affect the rate of reaction? predicting equilibrium conversion?" We might have many different goals.

3. The goals listed above are then recast into "observable" terms so that we can observe a person "demonstrating that they have achieved the goal." Part of this task is to remove ambiguity as to the conditions, constraints and form of evidence that would be expected. This usually means that we will add the words "Given...., you will be able to ..." Here are some suggestions to convert goals into an observable goal or set of subgoals:

   a. For desired actions choose verbs that are observable. Example 9-1 lists advice.
   b. Define any jargon terms.
   c. Recheck to see whether the objective is better expressed as "results" instead of "how" or "procedures."
   d. Usually we will have to specify the conditions (or "givens") under which the task is to be done.

   The resulting well-stated objective may not be our final version; we may have to revise it as we try to evolve criteria to tell us when we have reached the goal. This is discussed later.

Example 9-1 Suggested usage

DO NOT USE-   USE

- know   - describe
- feel   - construct
- understand   - calculate
- be aware   - determine
- plan   - show how to
- interpret   - list

---

4. Once a tentative description is given in step 3, we then think about the evidence that might be produced from that activity. State the evidence and ask "Is this realistic?."

5. The first four steps are about as far as we go now in creating the goals. However, this is only tentative. The goal statements will undoubtedly have to be revised to make them consistent with the *criteria*, the *feedback form expected*, the *resources*, the *type of evidence expected* and the *performance conditions*.

If you need more on this topic of creating observable goals, take time to read resources from the McMaster Problem Solving program supporting this book, MPS **3a** and **3**.

9.2-3 Created by Whom?

Since setting the goals is the key to everything, if you select incomplete or inadequate goals you learn the wrong material in terms of the "big picture" for the course or program. How can you be sure you have the **correct** goals?

Different PBL programs and courses take different approaches.
- Some provide global unit objectives (almost the same as a listing of the subjects, as in Table 9-3) and expect you to create detailed ones that satisfy you and yet fit within the big picture.

- Some PBL courses provide the Case problem and expect the tutor to provide feedback about the objectives you create. (This is done in some of the Guided Design programs.)

- Some PBL courses provide the global objectives and then give you feedback after you have created yours as to the appropriateness of your specific objectives. (This is the approach in the MPS SDL program.)

- Some PBL programs start the program with the faculty supplying global and specific objectives and then as the program progresses, you assume more responsibility for creating your own objectives. (Alverno College).

- Some give you specific objectives which, when you complete, gives you a "satisfactory" or "B" in the Unit. Students must create their own objectives to get "outstanding or "A." (The MPS program as a whole.)

- Some give you specific objectives throughout. (Michigan State and Mercer Medical school).

In summary, sometimes the objectives are issued from the program, sometimes they are created by the tutor, sometimes by the students, sometimes this is a shared responsibility. Determine who creates the objectives in your PBL program.

9.3 Selecting Criteria

Regardless of who creates the goals, I feel that the learning objectives must include the criteria. Criteria are the measures we use to decide if a goal has been achieved. For example, suppose our goal is to "earn some money." Such a statement is incomplete because we do not know how we would judge the meaning of "some." The **criterion** to tell us that the goal has been achieved might be "more than $50." Thus, we can monitor progress; "I now have $30, only $20 more!" We also can tell when the goal has been achieved: "I now have $55; I'm there!"

Criteria are easy to describe; some find them difficult to identify and express in measurable terms. Next we consider the characteristics of criteria, how to create them, who creates them and how the criteria are related to *standards*.

9.3-1 Characteristics of Criteria

Some characteristics of criteria are:

1. They must be related to the objective or to well-stated goals. For example, do not use *weight* as the criterion to decide which apple is the "reddest."

2. The criterion must be measurable. For example, to select the reddest apple we might initially look at colour standards or even colour wavelengths and agree on the standard

that a panel of judges deems to be the reddest. Then all apples are compared to the standard.

3. There may be inferred criteria that are not stated in the problem statement. For example, for the question "What is the composition of the blood going into the heart?," the criterion is unstated. We might infer different interpretations from the context. Thus, the criterion might be:

   a. That the composition of the major 10 components be specified (but we can neglect the trace species).

   b. That the data reported are accurate to within 2% (or that different accuracies will be given with each number reported).

   c. That the analyses need to be run in triplicate.

   d. That we need independent confirmation of the data from another laboratory.

4. Agreement must be reached about the criteria *before* the task is performed.

9.3-2 Creating Criteria

Some suggestions for the process of creating criteria are:

Option 1: Contrast the extremes. Describe what would be excellent; contrast with what would be failure. An example is given in Table 9-5.

Option 2: Arnold's **A**chieve, **P**reserve and **A**void method. Here we ask "What do we want to achieve? preserve? and avoid? in achieving the goal?" This approach applies best when we are deciding a course of action involving people or when we are deciding what to communicate.

Option 3: Be the Teacher. In this option, you pretend that you are the teacher who is asked to determine whether someone has "learned" something. How would you test? Create the test you would use.

9.3-3 Who Creates the Criteria?

Whoever creates the learning objectives should create the criteria because the two should go hand-in-hand. Indeed, criteria should be included in the statement of the objectives. Sometimes, you are given objectives without criteria. Here, you will

Table 9-5: Example: **participation**

We want to assess member's participation in the group meetings in PBL. What criteria would we use?

An Answer:

A listing of the characteristics of good participation might be: present, enthusiastic, willing to offer information and new ideas, provide statement relevant to the discussion, willing to ask for clarification, give feedback, attentive, summarize, praise, punctual, prepared, maintain on task.

A listing of the characteristics of poor participation: absent, late, unprepared, disruptive, bored, sleeping, looking out the window, silent or too aggressive, tells stories.

From these emerge pairs of descriptors that might be classified as Task: information seeker, information giver, summarizer, "timely" (attendance, punctuality, preparedness and meets deadlines) and task oriented "interpersonal skills". In addition there are Morale descriptors.

These can be quantified into measurable terms for each descriptor, or into a measurable scale for Task and Morale descriptors.

intuitively create your own criteria, but it would be wise for you to create written criteria and confirm these with the assessor. Initially, the criteria may be created by the instructor, by the program or by the tutor. However, gradually you, the learner, should acquire the skill.

In summary, criteria are very difficult to create. Yet, without criteria, the creation of the goals/objectives cannot be done well. Criteria and goal setting go hand-in-hand.

9.3-4 Standards and Expectations; Empowerment and Accountability

Whoever is empowered with the assessment needs to be accountable for the standards and quality of the overall experience. Being given the power to self-assess is **not** being given the licence to give yourself whatever rating you wish. You are accountable for your standards of performance. The standards and expectations should be on an absolute - not a relative - basis. That is, we are not interested in seeing who does better than someone else, or to establish a *ranking*. We are rating performance relative to some benchmark or standard of performance. Someone has to establish what that standard is.

You probably will include feedback from the tutor, early on, about the quality of the goals and the criteria that you set for yourself. Without doubt, the tutor will be assessing the quality of the *assessment process* you use. The expectations will vary depending on the knowledge or skill being assessed. For some, we might expect **zero** errors, 100%. For others, we might accept a range above a minimum benchmark: 50% as being acceptable or adequate and add descriptors like "more than adequate" and "outstanding." Other words include "fair," "good," "excellent." These can be converted to a numerical percentage. Another option is to provide a number of descriptors and then ask "the extent to which all of the descriptors are demonstrated." The words could include "none of these," "a few of these but major omissions," "most of these" and "all of these." An example is given in Table 9-6.
When we create the standards and the measurable

Table 9-6 Feedback about assessment

Goals: Content is well identified, goals are challenging and achievable, goals are written in observable terms, goals are unambiguous, the "given" conditions are specified.

None of these behaviours		Few of these behaviours but major omissions		Most features demonstrated		All of these behaviours
☐	☐	☐	☐	☐	☐	☐
1	2	3	4	5	6	7

Criteria: Criteria are consistent with the goals and are measurable and practical. The criteria are challenging and achievable.

None of these behaviours		Few of these behaviours but major omissions		Most features demonstrated		All of these behaviours
☐	☐	☐	☐	☐	☐	☐
1	2	3	4	5	6	7

Evidence: The type and quality of evidence gathered is consistent with the goals and criteria. The evidence has been gathered conscientiously over a long enough period of time. The evidence is well organized. The quality and extent of evidence is sufficient to allow me to judge the extent to which the goals have been achieved.

None of these behaviours		Few of these behaviours but major omissions		Most features demonstrated		All of these behaviours
☐	☐	☐	☐	☐	☐	☐
1	2	3	4	5	6	7

Process: The assessment process has been applied and as an independent assessor I concur with the decision as to the degree to which the goals have been achieved.

None of these behaviours		Few of these behaviours but major omissions		Most features demonstrated		All of these behaviours
☐	☐	☐	☐	☐	☐	☐
1	2	3	4	5	6	7

Strengths   Areas to work on

_____   _____
_____   _____
_____
_____
_____   from D.R. Woods, "How to Gain the Most from Problem-based Learning" (1994)

criteria, we may have to return to the objectives and modify these. We may have to consider the "benchmarks" we are expecting and check that these are reasonable considering the resources available.

9.4 What Resources?

The goals must be achievable; the criteria must be satisfied and achievable. If we are blind, we should not aspire to be an airplane pilot. If we have little artistic ability, then we shouldn't try to be an artist. These may sound like common sense. However, some still try.

Consider now goals in the context of PBL. To achieve the goals, we must have the time, access to information resources, and sufficient people in the learning group that the goal can be achieved.

Sometimes, for example, each member of the self-directed learning group will elect to learn a *different* concept and return to the group to teach the others the concepts. Other times, all group members will learn the *same* material and return to the group to compare notes and discuss the same issue. We need to identify some resources that are needed. Indeed we may have to revise the goals/objectives based on the resources. Are the goals realistic and attainable?

Goals are achievable

I make $30 000 per year now. Next year my goal is to make $200 000.

I know nothing about computers now, next year I want to be a world authority on PC Trieex computers.

Feedback

These may be well founded for some; for most these are unattainable.

Goals need to be realistic.

A feature of goals-that-are-attainable is that usually we are given complex cases and situations that we need to know an immense amount of knowledge. We have to create objectives that focus on the key knowledge needed and that we can learn with the resources available.

The key will be to learn the fundamentals first for the key and major issues illuminated by the Case. We need to apply the Principle of Successive Approximation. You can't learn it all in one Case!

9.5 What Constitutes Evidence?

From the goals or learning objectives we can gather an idea of the kinds of evidence we might provide to show that we have achieved the goal. Often in self-directed learning, the learner formulates the evidence. Sometimes, the feedback forms (such as those given in Table 3-5 (on Problem solving), Table 5-1 (for Group process), Table 5-5 (for Team dimensions) or Table 7-3 (on SDL-teach)) can be used as part of that evidence.

You should think of this ahead of time so that you can document and apply the criteria objectively. Ask:

- What type of evidence is applicable? how is the evidence related to the goals? and which criteria does it satisfy? In presenting evidence, feelings are fine, but quantitative data are preferred. Journal writing is a commonly used and very effective way of documenting achievement. Probably you will also keep a file where you place records of annual activities.

- What method of monitoring can I use to help me keep on track?

- Can I find about seven pieces of different validating evidence to support each claim for each goal?

Table 9-7 illustrates a case.

9.6 What is the Purpose for the Assessment?

We assess for some purpose. What is it? Table 9-8 lists some options. Why do you want to be assessed?

9.7 Under What Performance Conditions Will the Assessment be Done?

We need to understand the conditions under which the assessment is going to be done. Is it during the small group tutorial? Is it based only on the performance during the tutorial or does it include my self- and group assessment at the end of the session? Is it a separate written activity? Does it include my journal?

For self-assessment, one is tempted to suggest that the assessment is continual. Nevertheless, there are specific times when you will specifically think about your progress and the degree to which you have achieved the goals. Identify those times. More importantly, set aside time to do this.

9.8 Who Does the Assessment?

Many different people could assess: trained observers, peers, a peer identified to be an observer, the tutor, other groups, you, the simulated patient, a faculty member who will look at your work, peers who will look at your work. Maybe many different assessors. Whoever does the assessment should be familiar with the feedback forms and instruments and with the assessment process.

In self-assessment, you are empowered to do the assessment. You will be accountable to your peers, probably the tutor and to the program.

9.9 What Standard Forms are Used for the Assessment?

Whenever an instructor marks homework, she first creates a standard marking sheet that reminds her of the allocation of marks and what counts for part marks.

Similarly, for assessment, it helps with the objectivity, validity and mutual understanding of the assessment if:

- The assessor works with a standard form.

- Both the person being assessed and the assessor are familiar with and comfortable with the "feedback" form. Both should be aware of the limitations of the form.

The standard form should be created:

1. Based on the principles outlined in Chapter 5, Section 5.2-3, on "Growth through feedback: other guidelines toward interpersonal Shangri La." For example, feedback should identify the positives and identify the areas to work on. The feedback should be structured and successive. By this I mean that if a person has 25 things wrong, then *at this time* we identify the top two that should be worked on, and all of the others become OK temporarily. At the same time, we should identify the knowledge that is correct and the skills that are effective and in place.

2. Be pertinent to the content, goals and criteria.

3. Be easy to work with.

4. Include enough range that useful distinctions can be made.

5. Be objective and reliable. Feedback among independent observers should be consistent. One approach is to use a Likert scale that "makes a statement" and asks you to rate the degree to which you, the assessor, agree or disagree with the statement. An example of the Likert scale is given in Table 9-6.

Table 9-7: Example: **seeing progress in learning**

You are finding it difficult to see progress in your learning. You think you are doing OK but you wish you had a better sense of accomplishment. What might you do?

An Answer:

You might start a journal in which you note your starting skill before a session and then reflect on your personal assessment after the 1st week, after the 2nd and so on. You might identify particular personal goals you want to achieve, create a simple feedback form and ask members of your group to provide you with feedback. One of the keys is to identify the goal, reflect and record. In the sense of recording, it is useful to have a convenient and easy way to do this. For more on journal writing see Alverno College and the MPS program: Woods (1994) the instructor's guide or PS News **84** or **85**.

Some of the challenges about giving feedback are:

1. If the performance is below standard, then the observer tends to see only the 45 things that the person did wrong. The feedback provides **too** much, unstructured feedback. Usually little attempt is made to identify the strengths.

2. If the performance is well above standard, then the observer tends to be all positive and fails to identify areas to be worked on.

3. If the performance is below expectation, we usually prefer **not** to identify the fault. If we do not identify the area to work on, no growth can occur. Sometimes we will anecdotally describe the fault yet provide a "passing mark." Consider, for example, a workshop to improve the ability to create objectives. The

Table 9-8 Purpose for assessment

I want to be assessed so as to:

a) Provide feedback from a "tutor" and thus convince me that I have all the knowledge and skills they expect.

b) Provide feedback to me so that I can monitor and see progress.

c) Help me develop a valid self-image or self confidence of what I know.

d) Give certification for external agencies. "This "mark" proves that I am a qualified Pharmacist."

e) Provide criteria for admission into more advanced programs. "Give me a "mark" so that I can get into graduate school."

f) Develop my autonomy in learning.

g) Develop my skill in the process of doing a self-performance appraisal.

h) Provide a "mark" or "rating" of achievement as a summary of accomplishment.

i) Force me to put the whole course, or body of knowledge into perspective.

j) Give me confidence that I am learning something from the self-directed learning activity.

k) Other.

person you are observing cannot do the task. On the feedback form you note under areas to work on "learn how to create issues." Yet, when asked to give the student a "mark" you might say "Satisfactory." If you do this, then the person never does learn how to create objectives. Feedback is for growth. We cannot grow without objective and helpful feedback.

In general, one person should not be expected to observe and give feedback to more than about three persons at one time. (de Stephen, 1985; Swanson et al., 1991)

For self-assessment, you might create your own feedback/assessment forms.

9.10 When Are the Results of the Assessment Disclosed?

Promptly.

9.11 What are the Conditions Under Which the Results are Disclosed?

An interview or discussion between the assessor and the assessed is probably best. For self-assessment, you will probably assess yourself continually and set aside times when you reach milestones when a more formal approach is taken.

9.12 What Training in and Monitoring of the Assessment Process Occurs?

Training should be provided; being given the power to self-assess brings with it accountability for the result you publish from the assessment.

9.12-1 Training

Training in the process of assessment helps all involved. The McMaster Problem Solving program supporting this book, Unit MPS 3 is an example of such a training activity. This is described by Woods et al. (1988).

9.12-2 Monitoring: Empowerment and Accountability

We need to monitor the assessment process we use. We can self-monitor; use peers or ask to the tutor for input. Table 9-6 might provide a format for feedback.

9.13 Self-assessment

In self-assessment (in self-directed learning), all of the components discussed so far are part of the task: setting observable goals, identifying measurable criteria, matching the criteria to the goals, identifying activities to achieve the goals *and* providing evidence that the goals have been achieved. The distinguishing feature is the **you** are going to do the assessment and provide yourself with feedback.

9.14 Self-assessment in the Context of Self-directed, Interdependent, Small Group PBL

Self-assessment is a natural part of self-directed, interdependent, small group PBL. Being empowered to assess your own learning, your group process, your problem solving and your attack on the problem:

- Frees you from dependence on the tutor to answer the question "How well are we doing?"

- Nurtures your setting of personal goals that are richer than you might tackle otherwise.

- Helps develop trust and acceptance among your team members; shifts a group into a team. This is because you will be counting on team members to give you fair, objective constructive evidence to be used in your assessment.

- Gives a freshness and promptness of the feedback that might otherwise be missing.

- Helps develop your skill at assessment and the assessment process.

- Helps develop accountability because you know that the empowerment to self-assess is accompanied by accountability. This, in turn, develops the attitude of *how can I learn the most from my whole educational experience?*.

Being empowered to self-assess is awesome.

9.15 Understand the Role of the Tutor

Take time to determine the role of the tutor in the assessment process.

9.16 Summary and Feedback

Effective assessment of performance requires published, explicit observable goals and measurable criteria, an understanding about what constitutes objective evidence and the conditions under which the evidence can or should be collected. It also should be clear as to who will do the assessment and how the assessment will be presented. The 12 key components in any assessment are outlined. All conditions and components in the assessment process should be explicit and published.

Being empowered to self-assess does not give you licence to "give yourself what you want." You are accountable. The goals you set should be attainable and should stretch you. They should be consistent with those of the tutors and of the program. The criteria used to test that the goals have been achieved, and the evidence that you supply should be complete, pertinent, measurable and unambiguous. The assessment process you use should serve your stated purpose and be accountable to outside, independent scrutiny.

Table 9-6 gives a feedback form that you can use to reflect on the process you use to do an assessment.

For more, see MPS Unit **3**, Alverno (1985), Loacker and Jensen (1988), Boud (1988) and Woods et al. (1988). For more on assessment options for testing subject knowledge (if you wish to create "tests" that another PBL student group would use for feedback) see Swanson et al. (1991).

9.17 References

Alverno College (1985) "Assessment at Alverno College," Alverno College publications, 3401 S. 39th St Milwaukee, WI.

Arnold, J.D. (1978) "Make up your mind!" Amacom, 135 West 50th St., New York, NY.

Boud, D. (1988) "Assessment in Problem-based Learning," Assessment and Evaluation in Higher Education, **13**, 2, 87-91.

de Stephen, R., (1985) personal communication, Hilton Head Conference on Teaching Thinking.

Loacker, G., and P. Jensen (1988) "The Power of Performance in Developing Problem-solving and Self-assessment Abilities," Assessment and Evaluation in Higher Education, **13**, 2, 128-149.

MPS **3**, "Self-assessment," Chemical Engineering Department, McMaster University, Hamilton, ON.

PS News **84**, Jan-Feb 1993, ISSN 1180-5471, Department of Chemical Engineering, McMaster University, Hamilton, ON. [features MPS Unit **3**, "Self-assessment," with an example journal.]

PS News **85**, Mar-April, 1993, ISSN 1180-5471, Department of Chemical Engineering, McMaster University, Hamilton, ON. [features MPS Unit **5**, "Managing Stress," with an example journal.]

Swanson, D.B., S.M. Case and C.P.M. van der Vleuten (1991) "Strategies for Student Assessment," Chapter 27 in "The Challenge of Problem-based Learning," D. Boud and G. Feletti, eds., Kogan Page, London.

Woods, D.R., Marshall, R.R. and Hrymak, A.N. (1988) "Self-assessment in the Context of the McMaster Problem Solving Program," Evaluation and Assessment in Higher Education **12**, No. 2, p 107 to 127.

Woods, D.R. (1994) Instructor's Guide: "How to Help Your Students Gain the Most from PBL," Department of Chemical Engineering, McMaster University, Hamilton, ON. [includes a student journal on "strategy" and one on "self-directed learning."]

9-18 Exercises

9-1 Purpose of Assessment: Take 10 points and distribute them among the ten responses listed in Table 9-8 in a way that best reflects your feelings as to the purpose of assessment in the context of your course. If you feel that ten responses sum up your feelings, then assign 1 point to each response. The higher the points allocated, the more you feel this would be your response.

9-2 Identify one skill you have. Create the evidence you would use to show that you have achieved that skill. Exchange your writing with a classmate and give each other feedback.

10 *Putting it all together*

Saadia's PBL program

"My PBL program has very little structure. The tutor assigns a topic for us to study. The next class she has us to sit around a big table and "discuss". Since there are 35 in the class, I don't get much chance to discuss. Is this really PBL?" asks Saadia.

Sonja is puzzled too. However, her response is, "This certainly is better than passive lectures. Besides the topic "drives" my learning. In that sense, I see this as PBL. As for the other components and skills described in this book, my response is..".

What might Sonja say about Saadia's PBL program?

Self-assessed, self-directed, interdependent, small group PBL is an exciting environment for learning. Not all courses and programs will adapt it the same way. Wide variation exists among medical schools that claim to be problem-based. Travel from medical school to schools of nursing, occupational therapy, pharmacy, law, forestry, veterinary medicine and engineering and you will encounter great variation. Take Saadia's PBL program as an example. Sonja's initial response is insightful. How might she respond further?

For Saadia's situation, what do you know already about self-assessed, self-directed, interdependent, small group PBL?

Perhaps you already are skilled in self-assessed, self-directed, interdependent, small group PBL learning. If so, I trust that this book has helped you to make explicit the skills and attitudes needed for you to get the most from the program. If you know all of the issues and details for taking any PBL format or variation on that theme, and, making it work effectively for you, then please help others enrich their experiences. You might use this book as a framework around which to add your particular experience.

For this situation, what are the issues?

Some of the issues, for making the most with your particular format of PBL, are:

1. Be flexible. Expect variations in approach to PBL; learn to gain the most from each approach.
2. Embrace **all** the skills you are developing. See the experience as developing and polishing

Table 10-1 Some variations in PBL

Topic	Some Options in PBL			
	Guided Design	Medical School	Business School Case Approach	MPS Program
Problem description	About ½-1 page.	About 1 paragraph.	About 10-40 pages.	About 1 paragraph.
Feedback to the first step.	Tutor-generated, written feedback based on anticipated student response. Students get this when they are ready.	Tutor with group of five students asks questions and provides feedback.	Instructor facilitates student discussion in a class size of 30 to 80.	Groups have their written objectives and issues validated by tutor when they are ready.
Independent self-study	All study the same topic and bring to the group to discuss.	Variable: all may study the same or different subjects and bring this to group to "teach/learn" from each other.	Each studies issues and knowledge of the case and comes to class to describe and justify results.	All study different subjects and bring these to the group to "teach/learn" from each other.
Assessment	Tutor.	Predominantly tutor.	Tutor.	Self-assess with tutor monitoring the process via personal interview.

your skills in important areas beyond "learning the subject knowledge". These might include (depending on your context) problem solving, group process, self-directed and interdependent learning, lifetime learning and self-assessment skills. In addition you will undoubtedly be creating a structure in the knowledge that differs from what you would learn from a "subject-based" approach. Be aware of this and do the extras to consolidate the structure.

3. Successively enrich your skills.

4. Keep communication open.

5. Be patient.

6. Monitor and give each other frequent feedback.

7. Understand the role of the tutor.

Each of these issues is considered in turn. You may wish to go directly to the section that answers your needs.

10.1 Be Flexible: Expect, and Understand the Variations in Approach to PBL

Many different approaches are used. Table 10-1 illustrates just a few. In some approaches you will not be given an opportunity to "self-assess;" the

Table 10-2 Who is responsible for each activity in your PBL program?

Activity	Tutor	Shared	Student
Pick problem			
Identify issues			
Goals/criteria			
Pick resources			
Create assessment			
Do assessment			
Embed knowledge in problem			
Reflect on process			

tutor will do it all. That's OK. Don't focus on what opportunities that are missing. Focus on the opportunities you have.

To help appreciate those opportunities take time to identify who is responsible for each activity in the PBL process. Complete Table 10-2.

10.2 Embrace All the Skills

Your PBL format and experience offers you a chance to develop skills *other than acquiring new knowledge.* Some programs provide better opportunities than others; yet usually some opportunity arises to improve your skills in:
- problem solving,
- interpersonal relationships, listening and responding,
- self-awareness and self-confidence,
- group process,
- self-directed and independent learning,
- self-directed and interdependent learning (which I refer to as "lifetime learning" skills),
- self-assessment,
- relating subject knowledge to problems and their solution (which alters our "structure" of that knowledge in our LTM),
- extracting experience knowledge.

Use the Chapters in this book to provide a framework for the development of these skills.

10.3 Successively Enrich Your Skill

Apply the principle of successive approximation. Recall from Figures 2-2 and 2-3 that PBL tends to develop breadth of knowledge across a range of subjects and that that development is one of successively building more depth across the range of subjects. We need to resist the temptation to try to "learn it all" from one case problem. We gradually build up our knowledge. Similarly, you may have used this book as a guide to your first Problem. You have reflected on the change process you are working through, the problem solving skills that you are applying and so forth. However, the sets of skills related to problem solving, change management, group process, self-directed learning and self assessment are as complex and extensive as any other set of five subjects. In PBL you are simultaneously learning the subject disciplines and these five additional subjects. As cautioned frequently in this book

"You can't learn it all, all at once!"

Just as you build up knowledge in the subject discipline successively, so you can build up your skills in the five areas of attitude, problem solving, group skills, self-directed, interdependent learning and self-assessment successively. We wish we had **all** the skills developed at once. We can't! Rather, we can look at "Themes" to build up the skills successively. Table 10-3 offers suggestions about how to do this.

> For the first PBL activity; don't try to apply all the principles in this whole book; rather focus on being aware of some of the processes and monitoring what you are doing. Specifically, you might focus on Chapter 1, for attitude, the activities in Chapter 3 and some of the activities in Chapter 5. Emphasize reflection and awareness.
>
> In PBL activity 2, your second case problem, you might try two different themes: goal setting/defining problems and trying to relate the new subject knowledge to real-world and issues. Goals, goal setting, seeing different perspectives and points-of-view - these are crucial steps that influence:
> - problem solving: defining the real problem;
> - self-directed learning: the key is setting learning objectives;
> - assessment; without clearly-defined goals we cannot assess progress.

Similarly, other Themes and topics are outlined in Table 10-3 so that you build up your confidence and skill successively.

10.4 Keep Communication Open

Communicate with your tutor. Communicate with your classmates. Work cooperatively and, above all, share ideas and concerns about the process.

Communicate to yourself by reflecting on the process you use.

Writing a reflective journal or diary is probably the best way to develop your skills. Why? Most programs to elicit a change in attitude and to develop confidence use "reflective journal writing." (see, for example, Chamberlain, 1978). Your task is to write down your ideas, clarify them, make sense out of them, marshall the evidence, relate the evidence to the criteria and goals to see your progress. Monitor that progress until you achieve your goals and **know** that you have achieved them. What do you include? If you want some structure for journal writing you might:
- Assemble the goals and criteria.
- Reflect on how you did the task *before.*
- Reflect on the big picture of what you discovered because of the past events and activities.
- Analyze the evidence and draw conclusions that relate to your objectives. The result is "the degree to which the objectives have been achieved."
- Enrich your experience by explicitly trying to apply the skill in other contexts (school and everyday life). Provide evidence and reflect on the events.
- Reach some conclusions and set goals for future growth.

Example journals are published in PS News **84** (1993).

10.5 Be Patient

The skills are complex; you are developing them in the midst of uncertainty because of the newness of the whole adventure in learning. Be patient, especially with yourself.

10.6 Monitor and Give Each Other Frequent Feedback

You may feel uncertain. Your stress level high may be high. Remember the change process you are working through. Use the various feedback forms presented in this book to help you reflect and monitor your progress. Ask your colleagues to use the forms to provide you with prompt feedback.

Table 10-3 Learn the knowledge and skills successively

Subject knowledge	Problem solving skills	Interpersonal and group skills	Self-directed, interdependent skills or "lifetime learning skills"	Self- assessment skills or performance review skills	Attitudes
PBL activity 1: *Theme:* being aware and monitoring.	Strategies and monitoring. Form Table 3-5.	Fundamentals, Expectations and personal feedback via exercise 5.5 about what you do. Form Table 5-1.	Offer feedback form in Table 7-3.		Change process, attitude shifts needed.
PBL activity 2: *Themes:* Issues and goals; & Knowledge structure: tie to fundamentals via "issues.	Defining problems: using triggers in Table 3-6 to identify "issues.		Learning Goals: making them observable and adding measurable criteria.	Goals: making them observable and adding measurable criteria.	
PBL Activity 3: *Theme:* Self-talk.	Creativity: deferring judgement; self-talk; Triggers Table 3-2; Feedback Table 3-3.	Self-talk and anger. Personal preference: Jungian typology.			Self-talk and stress management.
PBL Activity 4: *Theme:* Criteria.	Criteria and decision-making; Table 3-4.		Measurable criteria for assessment of goals.	Measurable criteria for assessment: evidence.	
PBL Activity 5: *Theme:* Self management.	Exploring issues.	Coping with conflict.			Time management.
PBL Activity 6: *Theme:* Experience knowledge and pointers relating knowledge structure to real-world problem.	Decisions by consensus.	Chairperson.	Teaching versus presenting.		
PBL Activity 7:					
PBL activity 8:					

10.7 Understand the Role of the Tutor

For your particular version of PBL, clarify the role of the tutor.

10.8 Enjoy!

PBL is the richest learning environment you will probably encounter in your lifetime. Savour it and enjoy.

10.9 References:

Chamberlain, J. (1978) "Eliminating your SDBs: self defeating behaviours," Brigham Young University Press, Provo, UT.

PS News **84** (1993) bimonthly newsletter "Problem Solving News," published by the Chemical Engineering Department, McMaster University, Hamilton, Jan-Feb 1993.

10.10 Exercises

10.1   What are the issues in Saadia's situation?

10.2   What might Sonja say?

10.3   What are the issues in your PBL situation?

10.4   How might you make the most from your PBL program?

10.11 For More

Here are my favourite resources about PBL.

Barrows, H.S. and R.M. Tamblyn (1980) "Problem-based Learning: an approach to medical education," Springer Publishing Co., New York, NY.

Boud, D.J. (1985) "Problem-based Learning in Education for the Professionals," HERDSA, Sydney.

Boud, D.J. and G. Feletti (1991) "The Challenge of Problem-based Learning," Kogan Page, London

Bridges, E.M. (1992) "Problem-based Learning for administrators," ERIC Clearing house on Educational Management, University of Oregon, Eugene, OR.

Christensen, R.C. (1987) "Teaching and the Case Method," Harvard Business School, Harvard, MA.

Erskine, J.A., M.R. Leenders and L.A. Mauffwette-Leenders (1981) "Teaching with Cases," School of Business Administration, the University of Western Ontario, London, ON.

Harrisberger, L. et al. (1976) "Experiential Learning in Engineering Education," American Society for Engineering Education, Washington, DC.

"Pedagogue," a Newsletter, McMaster University Faculty of Health Sciences, Room 3N51, HSC, Hamilton, ON, L8N 3Z5, Canada.

"Probe," a Newsletter of the Australian Problem-based Learning Network, c/o PROBLAC, PO Box 555, Campbelltown, NSW 2560, Australia.

Wales, Charley, "Centre for Guided Design," West Virginia University, Morgantown, WV.

Walton, H.J. and M.B. Matthews (1989) "Essentials of problem-based learning," Medical Ed., **23**, 542-558.

Appendix

Feedback for the Perry Model

In Chapter 1, two questionnaires were given to help you reflect on your attitude toward learning, as modeled by Perry. How might you interpret your responses to those questionnaires?

Before considering the details, treat your responses to all questionnaires, and the interpretation, with a grain of salt. There are no right or wrong answers. Your feelings at the time when you completed the questionnaire and the wording of the questionnaire may lead you to responses that "do not represent you".

How do you use a questionnaire? Questionnaires are designed, and validated, to help us focus on one particular issue. These two questionnaires ask you to reflect on "what your attitude is toward the learning process?" "Who should be responsible for what?" "What aspects of learning environment help your learning and make it more enjoyable?" One way to address the issue is to just ask those questions and use Perry's model as a framework for reflection. The questionnaires have been designed to facilitate that process.

Gainen Questionnaire

At the end of the questionnaire, you are asked to sum the number of responses you made that were A, B, C or D for the eight questions. Thus, the total

of all your answers should be 8. For example, Linc's response was:

Sum (A) __1_   (B) _2___   (C) __3_
(D) __2__

To convert to a Perry scale, multiply the number of (A) responses by "2", the number of (B) by "3"; (C) x 4 and (D) x 5. Then express this as an average by dividing by 8.

In this example, the result is: $(1 \times 2) + (2 \times 3) + (3 \times 4) + (2 \times 5)/8 = 3.75$.

Interpretation: although on some issues Linc was lower and on some, higher, in general, Linc's attitude was close to that described somewhere between column 3 and 4 of Table 1-2 with a tendency toward column 4.

LP-II by Moore-Fitch

To interpret the Learning Preference-II questionnaire of Bill Moore and Peggy Fitch, calculate the arithmetic average of the second numeral coding each of the ten responses. Thus, if Linc checked "54 would let me learn from my classmates and peers", then one of the 10 numerals to average is **4**, the second numeral in the code.

Some Responses

Here are some typical distributions for third year
engineering students.

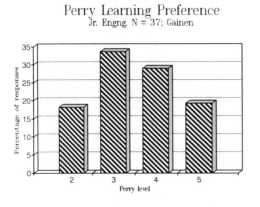

Perry Learning Preference
Jr. Engng. N = 37; Gainen

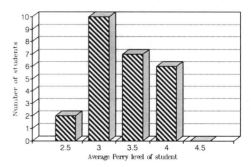

Perry Learning preference
Jr. Engng. N = 25 LP–II

Feedback forms

Some of the major feedback forms are given here for convenience:

- General awareness and skill for the process skills

- Problem solving (Table 3-6, p. 3-21)

- Group skills (Table 5-1, p. 5-9)

- Assessment skills (Table 9-6, p. 9-10)

- Self-monitoring of stress management skills (Table 1-5, p. 1-9)

- Self-directed learning skill (Table 7-3, p. 7-15)

Monitoring progress with processing skills (rate your awareness & skill at the end of each session, or week, on a scale from 0 [very low] to 10 [highest])

Processing skill	rating of Awareness				rating of Skill			
	1	2	3	4	1	2	3	4
Change management and stress: anticipate and describe stages, identify stages of anger and withdrawal and move through these, identify cause of confusion, explore corrective actions, implement and reflect and manage impatience; manage stress by worrying only about elements under your control, use positive self-talk, keep situation in perspective and has positive activities to relax and maintain health and sparkle.								
Problem solving: aware of process, uses a variety of methods, emphasis on accuracy, active, monitors and reflects, organized and systematic, flexible and sees situation from many different perspectives, objective and critically assess information, welcomes challenge, spend time defining problems, uses fundamentals, and uses explicit criteria for decision-making								
Interpersonal and group skills: as a group addresses Task: problem defined, explored, alternatives considered, criteria identified, task completed and look back and checked. Monitoring occurred. Task completed on time. Group avoids contributing excessive and irrelevant information; sticks to main themes without meaningless side tasks; **and** Morale: group is relaxed, enjoyed working together, gave emotional support to each other and were able to express disagreement or disappointment directly. members enthusiastic and involved.								
Team skills: maintenance of group attributes plus evolution of a group to develop team goals and willingly foregoes personal goals for the benefit of the team, each knows, accepts and performs role, decisions by consensus, conflicts are resolved so that 2+2 = 7								
Chairperson skills: prepares and distributes detailed agenda, does the necessary detail work ahead of time so as to have a "team event", facilitates the meeting [knowing when to be neutral and when proactive facilitation skills are needed]								

Monitoring progress with processing skills (rate your awareness & skill at the end of each session, or week, on a scale from 0 [very low] to 10 [highest])

Processing skill	rating of Awareness				rating of Skill			
	1	2	3	4	1	2	3	4
Self-directed, interdependent learning: aware of educational fundamentals and uses these to teach others, sets explicit learning objectives that have measurable criteria to identify achievement and that are achievable with the resources available, considers wide range of learning resources and willing to draw on peers as resources, agonizes through difficult parts of the subject [instead of skipping these and hoping they are not pertinent], creates forms of evidence to show accomplishment and applies these to both the knowledge learned and the process used.								
Self-assessment: knows and applies the issues in assessment, explores evidence of current and of target knowledge/skills, identifies goals for growth and converts these to observable objectives and measurable criteria, identifies the type of evidence needed to show accomplishment and systematically and critically gathers that evidence over a sustained period of time, makes adjustments as needed, searches for and uses both positive and negative feedback, and makes a judgement based on the evidence, criteria, objectives and goals that is deemed, by an outside evaluator, to be consistent, objective and valid.								
Knowledge structure: embeds new knowledge by applying it to solve the problem and elaborates and extends, identifies key "pointers" that link the theory to practice, identifies basic underlying fundamentals and relates new applications and uses to past experience. Asks "where else?" Knows the limitations of the knowledge.								
Experience knowledge: identifies and memorizes a wide range of tacit numerical values, processing procedures and rules of inference for the knowledge.								
Principle of successive approximation: is selective and able to identify **key** new knowledge and skill needed to solve the problem, does not try to learn "everything" when the resources are not available, is able to identify the next layer of information that would be tackled with more resources; patient and willing to let the knowledge and skill build up layer by layer.								

Attribute		Assessment
Awareness	+ can describe processes, can distinguish "exercise solving" from "PS."	
	- unaware of process; it's intuitive; cannot define a framework for PS.	
Variety of PS skills	+ can apply a variety of methods and hints.	
	- knows very few techniques; attempts to use a "one-step" solution.	
Emphasis on accuracy	+ checks, double checks, rechecks; concern for accuracy.	
	- concern for speed; unwilling to check.	
Active	+ writes things down, makes lists, prioritizes, makes tables and sketches;	
	- thinks in head, can't keep track, stares at paper.	
Monitors & reflects	+ assesses continually, assesses potential of ideas & options; continually evaluates and curtails; asks "where is this getting me?"	
	- does not monitor or assess; just does something.	
Organized & systematic	+ plans, anticipates, develops and uses a systematic plan.	
	- trial & error, impulsive, jumps around; no plan.	
Flexible & sees OPV	+ keeps options open; sees different points-of-view, willing to discard.	
	- quickly becomes fixed on one or two ideas or options even when mounting evidence proves these to be untenable; unwilling to discard.	
Use of knowledge: objective & critically assesses	+ objective, learns from others, critically assesses data.	
	- fails to draw on past experience, egocentric, assumes & believes everything they are told; accepts all information without question.	
Welcomes challenge	+ identifies disequilibrium as good; welcomes change and confusion.	
	- considers confusion to be "bad."	
Time allocation	+ spends most of time in exploring, defining, planning and engage stages.	
	- spends most time doing, calculating, writing.	
Overall approach	+ based on fundamentals, underlying principles, needs & goals.	
	- searches for sample solutions & cooks to try to make them work.	
Decision-making	+ applies criteria, draws conclusions substantiated by evidence.	
	- makes a selection based on "gut" reaction.	

Strengths   Areas to work on

_____   _____

_____   _____

_____

_____

_____ from D.R. Woods "How to Gain the Most from PBL," 1994.

Table 5-1 Feedback about roles in a group

			Group Members							
Task										
Observer -	Task Process	Orients group, monitors, summarizes, seeks direction, identifies phases +								
		Ignores phases, asks whatever wants, blocks, unaware of contributions -								
Giver -	Information Opinion	Assertively gives information, makes suggestions +								
		Withholds information, silent, aggressive or passive								
Seeker -	Information Opinion	Asks questions/for opinion; checks comprehension +								
		Refuses to ask for information, silent -								
Energizer -	Risk Taker	Enthusiastic, introduces spark, novel ideas +								
		Follower, agrees, silent, unsure -								
Morale										
Observer -	Interpersonal Process	Sensitive to interpersonal dynamics, comments on +								
		Ignores conflicts and tension, hopes it disappears -								
Giver -	Praise, Support	Warm, responsive, gives help, rewards +								
		Put downs, aggressive, self-centered, defensive -								
Seeker -	Interpersonal Problem Solver	Mediates, harmonizes, helps resolve conflicts +								
		Causes problems, seeks personal goals -								
Energizer -	Tension Relief	Jokes, laughs, shows satisfaction +								
		Withdraws, causes tension -								

from D.R. Woods. "How to Gain the Most from PBL." (1994)

Table 9-6 Feedback about assessment

Goals: Content is well identified, goals are challenging and achievable, goals are written in observable terms, goals are unambiguous, the "given" conditions are specified.

None of these behaviours		Few of these behaviours but major omissions		Most features demonstrated		All of these behaviours
☐	☐	☐	☐	☐	☐	☐
1	2	3	4	5	6	7

Criteria: Criteria are consistent with the goals and are measurable and practical. The criteria are challenging and achievable.

None of these behaviours		Few of these behaviours but major omissions		Most features demonstrated		All of these behaviours
☐	☐	☐	☐	☐	☐	☐
1	2	3	4	5	6	7

Evidence: The type and quality of evidence gathered is consistent with the goals and criteria. The evidence has been gathered conscientiously over a long enough period of time. The evidence is well organized. The quality and extent of evidence is sufficient to allow me to judge the extent to which the goals have been achieved.

None of these behaviours		Few of these behaviours but major omissions		Most features demonstrated		All of these behaviours
☐	☐	☐	☐	☐	☐	☐
1	2	3	4	5	6	7

Process: The assessment process has been applied and as an independent assessor I concur with the decision as to the degree to which the goals have been achieved.

None of these behaviours		Few of these behaviours but major omissions		Most features demonstrated		All of these behaviours
☐	☐	☐	☐	☐	☐	☐
1	2	3	4	5	6	7

Strengths   Areas to work on

_____   _____
_____   _____
_____
_____
_____   from D.R. Woods, "How to Gain the Most from Problem-based Learning" (1994)

Table 1-5 Monitoring checklist for stress management

Ideas	Not for me	Might work	OK	Use now
1. Worry only about things over which you have control				
2. Take care of yourself: exercise, eat and sleep regularly				
3. Use destimulating activities: deep breathing, muscle relaxation				
4. Use positive, **not** negative, self-talk: Rate your self-talk: don't know very negative neutral very positive				
5. Plan ahead				
6. Rename the stressful event: don't know use anxious name neutral "thing" positive				
7. Have a support system of family and friends. don't know have none few some many Have support system of traditions don't know have none few some many				
8. Use positive addictions that take your mind away to another world: music, hot bath, crafts, hobbies				
9. Be decisive				
10. Put it into perspective: "It's not the end of the world!"				
11. Use role models who have succeeded. don't know have none few some many				
Current stress: Symptoms	none	few	some	many
As measured by Holmes-Rahe (1967) or Holmes Gmelch (1983)	<100	101-300	301-500	>501

Table 7-3 Feedback for interdependent, self-directed learning

---

Feedback to _____ for Unit _____ Date _____

Present & on time: ☐   Present but late by ___ min.   Absent ☐

Quality of Knowledge: good intellectual understanding of the topic, the material supplied was complete and appropriate.

None of these.	A few but major omissions.		Most of these.		All of these.	
O	O	O	O	O	O	O

Quality of Instruction: he/she was here on time, the presentation was focused on the new knowledge; good choice of material and medium with effective communication and resource material supplied.

None of these.	A few but major omissions.		Most of these.		All of these.	
O	O	O	O	O	O	O

Followup: from this presentation I will have to:

Must study subject on my own; I learned nothing from your presentation.	Major self-study needed. I have some starting references from your presentation.	Some self-study of the basics.		No self-study of the basics. I want to r e f l e c t about the ideas.	
O	O	O	O	O	O

Strengths   Areas to Improve on

_____   _____

_____   _____

_____

_____

_____   from D.R. Woods. "How to Gain the Most from PBL." (1994)

Author Index

Annotated Subject Index

Teacher-guided learning: responsibility for the required elements in learning is shared between the teacher and the students. Contrast with Student-directed.
- and Arnie's group, Professor Ego, 6-1;
- and student's dependence on, 6-1;
- comparing with other options, 2-2, 2-3, 6-2;
    - illustrative table with options, 2-3;
- listing of issues, 6-2, 6-3, 10-3;
        - example, 6-5;

Teacher, be the, as a method of creating criteria, 9-8;

Teaching, the process of facilitating the learning of knowledge and skills. see Learning.
- student's role as teacher in self-directed, interdependent learning, 6-4;
    - list of tasks, 6-2; Table 6-2, 6-3;
    - identifying tasks in your version of PBL, Ex 6.2, 6-5; 10-3;

Team (and team work)
- and assessment to develop, 9-14;
- comparison with group, 4-2; 5-15, Table 5-4, 5-16;
- feedback form for growth, 5-17;
- how to build, 5-15;
- moving through disclosure, conflict resolution and trust, 5-15; 9-14;
- target skills, 5-17;
- to facilitate learning, 4-1;

Themes: major themes in this book:
- build up your knowledge and skill through successive development in both the subject knowledge and the process skills such as attitude, problem solving, group skills, self-assessment and self-directed, interdependent learning; you can't learn it all immediately; 2-3, 3-5, 10-3;
- have explicit, observable **goals** (for confidence, for managing stress, to remove the ambiguity in assessment, to function well in self-directed learning, to focus energies, to successfully solve the real problem) 3-20;
- have measurable criteria consistent with the goals, 3-20;
- improving any skill does not occur if we just try doing it in an unstructured fashion. We improve by taking the skill apart into component tasks, do the task, get feedback to see how you performed the task, reflect, learn from research evidence as to how the task should be done, set goals and work toward those goals. 3-20;
- listing, Preface, x;
- monitor and reflect on the processes; journal writing, 3-20;
- this book is a *framework* of issues and ideas; very busy and complicated looking diagrams are shown illustrating the issues; resources are listed for further study **as you need it**.

Thinking: (cognition) using the mind.
- list of skills needed in problem solving, 3-11;
    - target skills for problem solving, 3-21;
- taxonomy for the development of (Bloom), 7-6, 7-7;

Thought processes:
- listing of some of those needed in the stages in solving problems, 3-10, 3-11;

Time management,
- for goal setting:
    - and "defining problems", 3-6;
    - and "Explore" versus "Do it", 3-21;
- for problem solving:
    - and "defining problems", 3-6;
    - and "Explore" versus "Do it", 3-21;
    - and reading, Larkin, 3-6;
    - comparison of time spent for different stages in the MPS problem solving strategy, 3-24;
- how to increase skill, 1-6;
- in a meeting, 5-12;
    - Sandler's 20 min rule for meeting, 5-12;
- learning about its relationship with stress, 1-5, 7-3;

Trial and error,
- as a tactic to develop a plan, 3-10;

Triggers: some event that starts another.
- to brainstorm, 3-14;
- to identify issues in a situation, 3-18;
- to help explore, 3-18;
- that initiate anger, 1-4, 1-5, 1-10;

Trouble shooting,
- example of PBL, 2-2, 3-17;

Trust: vital element in relationships.
- as a component in interpersonal skills, 5-2;
- as shift from "group" to "team," 5-17, 9-14;

Working backwards,
>   - as a tactic to develop a plan for problem solving, 3-10;
>   - as a characteristic of "problem solving", 3-5;
>   - contrast with working forwards, 3-5;
>   - guess and work backwards, to prioritize issues, 3-187;

Working forwards,
>   - as a characteristic of "exercise solving", 3-4;
>   - contrast with working backwards, 3-5;

Workshops:
>   - as option for learning, 2-3;
>   - characterized by organization and responsibility, 2-3;
>   - example workshops to:
>>   - develop organizational awareness in problem solving, 3-23;
>>   - develop awareness of group skills, 5-19;
>   - listing of ones available to support this book, see "MPS Units."

WSY What's stopping you? 3-18;